Communities

at

War

Communities

at

War

DEFENDING OUR SCHOOLS, HOSPITALS, AND
HOUSES OF WORSHIP IN THE 21ST CENTURY

R.J. Godlewski

Chief Executive Manager at Tactical Extractions, LLC.

*"A prophet is not without honor except in his native
place and among his own kin and in his own house."*
Mark 6: 4 *NAB*

Communities at War: Defending our Schools, Hospitals, and Houses of Worship in the 21st Century

Copyright © 2015, R.J. Godlewski

Printed by Createspace Independent Publishing Platform

ISBN-13 978-1480144859
ISBN   1480144851

Frontispiece image: © Sue Colvil - Fotolia.com

Warning: All individual security and personnel protection activities involve risk or injury, to oneself and to others, and great care must be exercised in carrying out any such activities. Expert legal and technical guidance should be consulted and equipment checked for reliability before any activities described within this book are carried out. The publisher, the author, or any affiliated party cannot assume responsibility for damage to property or injury, death or loss to persons that may result from carrying out the activities described within this book. In carrying out such activities described within this book, persons do so entirely at his or her own risk.

ACKNOWLEDGMENTS

To God the Father, the Son, and the Holy Spirit, without Whom I would find no talent, no opportunity, and no friends with which to affect either my trade or my interests.

Deo gratias.

DEDICATION

*To all who devote his or her life to defeating evil,
wherever it may be found, and protecting innocent
human lives wherever they may live.*

IN MEMORY OF

*To all who have lost their lives because society denied
them an opportunity to defend themselves.*

PREFACE

OURS is a world falling apart. Families no longer matter at best and officials continually redefined them at worst. Police officers are being restrained from protecting their communities and cities erupt into flames because some residents decide that *their* lives matter more than everyone else's does. Our entertainers and athletes promote disruptive lifestyles and politicians do everything humanly possible to squash employment opportunities and access to personalized healthcare.

In spite of this – or, more likely because of this – rest individuals whose commitment to kill retains no limitations or inhibitions of action. For a myriad of reasons undecipherable to most people, these individuals will kill, maim, and steal for no other reason than that he or she *can*. While we step back aghast over the "latest" atrocity, someone else will seek to capitalize upon, and even surpass, the notoriety of that most recent perpetrator.

For the most part, communities within the West, particularly the United States, have been shielded from this reality, but such beliefs are illusionary at best. In fact, the United States holds no honor amongst the believers in utopia, nor does any nation for that matter. Concepts such as utopia, nirvana, paradise remain temporal expectations of eternal bliss. Even Christian Heaven remains a place where no eye has seen, no heart has envisioned.

Earth is not Eden, nor is it necessarily spiritual; it remains the physical home of physical creatures. In the animal world, these creatures often fight and kill for survival and position. In the human world, people add various *desires* to these twin needs. For example, an otherwise compassionate individual will kill for sexual gratification, narcotics addiction, and a host of other psychological disturbances that question our concept of sanity. Nevertheless, being psychologically "disturbed" is *not* the same thing as being insane. For matters of colloquial discussion, most people that commit massacres, including a great many active shooters, are *not* insane people.

Neither Adolf Hitler nor Josef Stalin, it could be argued, were "insane" persons. On the other hand, Roman emperors Caligula and Nero probably were. Colombian narcotics kingpin Pablo Escobar, despite killing a significant number of people, remained exceedingly ruthless, but it is questionable whether he held any deep-seated psychological problems. Libyan strongman Muammar Qaddafi would have even fit the Pope's definition of "mad dog", a somewhat unfortunate classification made by U.S. President Ronald Reagan: "mad" *dogs* do not send weapons to other brutal canines.

What this discussion tells us is that murder and mayhem – often at the highest degrees of perpetration – come from *both* psychotic individuals and others less psychologically unbalanced. We may quip that "Only an *insane* individual could do such a thing!" but Dr. Stanley Milgram of Yale University proved in the 1960s that *sixty-five percent* of the human population could kill another innocent soul with very little prompting from an authority figure. Subsequent research bears this out.

Can we, then, claim that more than six people out of every ten are mentally disturbed, deranged individuals? No, of course not. But it does say that these six people *may* pose a threat to you and your community. We simply do not know *which* individuals are likely to haul off and start killing one another. What we can do, however, is perhaps, explain what that "authority figure" could represent: Evil. Call it the Devil, Satan, Lucifer, or simply rap music, perhaps, but *something* outside of ourselves causes otherwise rational and respectable beings to conduct great atrocities.

What this "thing" is not, however, is *supernatural*. It remains a created force just like butterflies and wildebeests. For Christians, Jews, and Muslims, the archenemy of humanity remains Satan – a diabolical angel, but a *creature* nevertheless. Where his power comes from is through a spiritual being's superior intelligence and the abundance of human weaknesses brought upon us by our bodies. For those who do not believe in religion, the question remains *what* causes otherwise decent people to do bad things and *who*, precisely, is perfectly qualified to diagnose these individuals both *before* and after he or she commits great harm.

As proven by the great multitude of suicide bombers that work the planet, there is just no way to understand *why* a university-educated man or woman with children will toss everything aside and blow themselves apart just to kill people they do not know. Analytical psychiatry simply cannot answer the question universally. Therefore, we must accept the *superhuman* – the presence of a force or a being greater in intelligence and strength but less in kindness and love than we human beings.

For the purposes of this book, we shall dispense with debate and simply refer to this hindering force as Evil and acknowledge that regardless of laws and regulation, regardless of analyses and diagnoses, and regardless of preferences and probabilities, *some individuals* will conduct great crimes against his or her fellow man. Sometimes, even, they will join packs of like-minded people who blanket their actions with a system of religion, politics, nationality, race, or culture to kill and maim en masse.

Our role is simple, we must *defend* ourselves and our *communities* against these individuals no matter what our personal beliefs and upbringing may desire us to do instead. To acquiesce to others or public authority will not suffice; economics and raw numbers are not in our favor. This book, then, represents your game plan for turning the tide against *whoever* tries to destroy your particular community...

TABLE OF CONTENTS

1. INTRODUCTION

WHEN faced with a threat, a person bears only one of four possible options: to flee, to fight, to posture, and to surrender. To flee simply means to run. To posture involves inflating the image of that individual in the hope that an aggressor becomes scared of the sight and runs away. Everyone has seen a cat's posture when confronting an unknown threat – they hiss loudly and arc their back, while the hair stands erect. It scares most humans, though we know that we could simply kill the cat with little effort.

Surrendering requires no explanation; it involves the process of turning one's life and possessions over to the aggressor. When law enforcement personnel, for instance, inform us to give our prized possessions to thieves because our lives are more valuable than mere possessions, we surrender a little of our dignity. After all, once we turn our belongings over to the attackers, how do we *know* that they will not harm us anyway? Alternatively, how will we feel if we discovered that although we may have been set free, the *next* victim was not as lucky? Just because we were not killed during the robbery does not mean that our assailants were not hardcore murderers after all.

Another consideration that must be addressed

is that if we submit, flee, or even posture, what happens *next time*? Will running only lead to a barrier? Will posturing not terrify a stronger attacker? Will our luck with submission run out? The final option – to fight back – holds its own litany of problems. For example, what do we fight back *with*? Our hands? A gun? A garbage can lid upside the head? And what happens if the attacker can withstand an impact from our hands, a bullet from a gun (people can be shot *several times* and still retain sufficient mobility to kill you – it is not like in the movies!), or a strike from that lid?

In order to live, one must fight. In order to *survive*, one must learn to increase his or her fighting abilities. That is, we must continually train, learn, and condition ourselves to be the "strongest" participant in any encounter with death. And this is *not* easy. The human body is exceptionally fragile; the human mind even more so. If an aggressor targets you for attack, then it is likely because he or she has singled you out as weak, vulnerable, or incapable. *Something* about you suggests an easy target to zero in on and you may not understand precisely what that is.

As most people remain oblivious to his or her surroundings, few realize the image he or she transmits to the broader world. No one ever believes that they go through life with a major target tattooed on their back, but this is the way they act. Few individuals gaze upon their surroundings from a spherical perspective; most concentrating on that relatively tiny 'tunnel' that exists directly in front of their eyes. The rest of their attention is devoted to smart phones, tablet computers, video games, lunch, that cute individual walking across the street, children, and what he or she plans on wearing during the next *deserved* vacation.

Criminals capitalize upon this lack of awareness. They also employ information that *you* provide them, going through parking lots to ascertain which vehicle owners have children (by way of those honor student bumper stickers), which theaters are least protected (by way of those asinine 'gun free zone' placards), and whose purse to steal (by way of, say, an elderly grandmother distracted with children). That criminals may be opportunistic in nature does not mean that he or she does not actively *seek* out opportunities.

If ours is a dangerous world, then it has to be that way because it remains an exceedingly careless world too. Far too many people place his or her care in the hands of other individuals whom he or she may have little information about them. For instance, how many parents place their children into elementary school – let alone preschool – without evaluating the facility, much less the teachers, janitors, etc.? As a society, we simply place too much trust in others to do what *we* should be doing instead.

In a similar manner, individuals place a great deal of information about themselves online, expecting for rather incredulous reasons that *only those they permit* will gaze upon these photographs, musings, and tirades about last night's dinner partner. Unfortunately, to copy that famous Las Vegas, Nevada advertisement, what happens on the Internet *stays* on the Internet. Twenty years after a youthful escapade, an individual may find him or herself dutifully married with a family and yet, *someone* somewhere we discover that caper and will either disseminate the information freely (thereby ensuring that it remains fresh enough for that individual's family to discover) or, perhaps, blackmail the victim because of it.

Within the larger context, many employees post photographs of their workplace on the Internet, perhaps even videos, and not a small population has gone as far as to recreate his or her office in alternative reality sites such as *Second Life*. What this means is, that any astute competitor, criminal, or terrorist can now freely plan his or her attack safely within cyberspace. And corporate executives and security personnel have absolutely no clue about a pending attack that may destroy that company's future and kill many of its employees.

Regrettably, the common thread here is that criminals and terrorists remain alert and manipulative whereas the vast majority of individuals remain rather foolish in *everything* that he or she does. This is partly due to a convenience-driven society where, nowadays, smart refrigerators will send out text messages to someone to buy an extra gallon of skim milk. Not to mention automobiles that can parallel park by themselves, effectively eliminating one of the requisites for obtaining a driver's license in the first place.

We cannot lay blame *completely* upon conveniences in society, however, for that society itself has evolved into a world where few learn to use that technology properly. The Internet, for instance, was designed so that academic and research institutions could share information quickly and securely without worrying about outages in one particular node or another. The system simply could not be disrupted unless the whole package was destroyed.

Today's World Wide Web serves this original purpose rather remarkably as diverse students and businesses can share data quickly and reliably, shedding months (if not years) off the old method of networking through the postal service. Point of fact, a high school graduate can now earn both undergraduate and advanced university degrees without drifting away from his or her desk. No more commutes to school, no more significant gaps of time between classes. And the trend extends beyond education too.

By some estimates, as many as sixty-percent of new jobs being created within the United States involve working at home from computer to some degree. That is simply astounding. With the advent of micro robotics, it will not be very long before *all* jobs – even production line industrial positions – will be orchestrated from home. And herein is where this modern society of ours takes all of this wondrous technology and shoots itself in the midsection.

Instead of using this capability to better ourselves, we simply dilute our minds and abuse our bodies. Computers become not tools for success, but mechanisms for shortening the evolutionary nature of that success. For instance, instead of developing athletic bodies, we are now concerned with playing fantasy sports in order to defeat our friends or, perhaps, make a few bucks on the side. Instead of watching documentaries to learn, how to do things for ourselves, we use the Internet to provide an avenue in which we can slander our enemies and speak behind our friends' back.

Instead of promoting our accomplishments and seeking new opportunities, we cannot go a moment without informing the world that our baby has to have its diaper changed *immediately*. Ours is a lost culture and it is not forsaken because we have lost guidance – and we have since we no longer seem to produce any effective leaders today – , we have lost our *own way* because it remains so much more appealing to emulate comic relief than it is to copy *true* success stories. We just no longer seem to be able to determine what is worth keeping and what is not.

2. HUMAN VALUE

PEOPLE often declare that money cannot buy happiness. At face value, this sentiment matches our cultural expectations rather admirably. However, two key observations quickly destroy this time-honored dictum. First, most people making such claims possess neither happiness nor money. Secondly, we have to clarify what we mean by the term 'happiness'.

In the first regard, a poor person stating that money cannot buy happiness is just that, a *poor* person; not simply someone without money or a way of making that money. After all, there are a great many people living in thatched huts in Africa that seem a lot happier than their counterparts living comparatively luxuriously in New York City. That a great many New Yorkers on the lower economic rungs appear just as dissatisfied with life seems to suggest that having or not having money remains inconsequential. This brings us to defining *happiness*.

Is happiness the unobstructed path to one doing as he or she pleases? Does it simply represent being content or pleased with one's lifestyle? Or does it mean a great deal more? Let us, therefore, make a rather straight declaration; that "happiness" represents joy in one's life, through the ability to do as one's conscience expects, while never remaining fully content so that that person may seek greater joys in the future (being 100% happy all of the time would seem rather boring for an evolutionary species such as ours). Where the distinction rests, remains with appreciation. That is, do we *appreciate* what we have and how we experience the world surrounding us?

Let us imagine, for a moment, that you are sitting at your dinner table alone and friendless for years. Before you realize it, a burglar breaks in through your window and points a gun towards your head. As you scream in terror, the dumbfounded criminal replies, "*Why* are you screaming? You should be *glad* to have someone to talk to!" How would this make you feel? Would being alone and friendless mean that you should give up your valuables, or possibly your very life, just to have a friend? Of course not.

The concept of money and wealth deals with appreciating that abundance – not ignoring it into a sin or curse. The reason that many heretofore-poor entertainers and athletes (not to mention all those Lotto winners) end up broke and impoverished is that he or she did not – perhaps, could not – appreciate wealth as an *effort*. With riches accumulated relatively quickly, he or she simply has not had sufficient time to process the wealth building strategies of the truly wealthy. Just because someone, say, enters a marathon race does *not* mean that he or she represents a runner – let alone a winner. Simply that he or she may be parroting the actions of those whose presence within the race implies months and years of conditioning and training.

We can transfer this analysis to the human perspective as an *individual* and society as a whole. What we gain out of life is based upon a simple formula:

EFFORT + *RESILIENCE* + *KNOWLEDGE* + *COMMON SENSE* + *LUCK* = *SUCCESS*

From this equation, we can make some rather extraordinary realizations. First, *any* success requires hard work, though that effort may not always be readily apparent. Some seemingly quick successes are actually built upon years' worth of failure and ancillary responsibilities. This brings us to the second item, resilience. If you cannot handle failure, you are doomed within this world. Many of those quick-rich actors and entertainers have never faced financial ruin before and, therefore, simply cannot manage their money effectively. And being born without money is *not* financial ruin; it is financial absence.

The third unit of the above equation represents knowledge and, usually, requires some intelligence on the part of the individual. To work hard towards a particular goal and remain true to course requires some degree of knowledge about the signposts and paths encountered along the way. To perceive this, does require some intelligence on the part of the individual, otherwise he or she will miss the signals. A person reading a map, for instance, has to decipher what the markings mean and understand the language before he or she recognizes value in their assistance.

Next, we come to that oft-neglected virtue of *common sense*. A short weakling is *not* going to win a weightlifting contest against an established contender. Nor would a blind person win a standard poker game. Unfortunately, modern society is doing *everything* possible to dismiss such common sense. In fact, it is now considered blasphemous to deny championship trophies to *all* participants or simply to call a slow runner out at first base during baseball games. This leads us to the final element of the Equation for Success.

Luck is, perhaps, the most ignored concept in human civilization. Sometimes, people succeed (in smaller endeavors) through sheer dumb luck. We have all observed this at one time or another. During a recent (2015) Detroit Lions – Seattle Seahawks football game, a Lions' receiver failed to achieve the winning touchdown as time was running out because he fumbled the football with only about a foot to go to reach the end zone.

More to home, you may have stood in line at the local Department of Motor Vehicle office for hours simply because you had picked the wrong day or the wrong hour to arrive at that location. We cannot always *control* every aspect of our lives. A man would have been working in the World Trade Center on the morning of September 11, 2001 had his grandmother not passed away a few days earlier and her funeral took the place of his work day. *Luck.* A father missed being broadsided by a speeding truck because he had dropped his car keys in the parking lot and was thus a few minutes late heading home. *Luck.*

Sometimes, in life, good things happen to the unprepared and bad things happen to the gifted. We just have to take such things in stride. That said, luck remains the *last* element within the equation – and for a good reason. If we work hard, keep at our task, learn as much about our world and ourselves as possible, and then retain common sense, all those annoying *luck* episodes will not defeat our mission. After all, we cannot be certain that "luck" is simply another way of accommodating for our primal survival instincts long since abandoned when modern conveniences took away our ability to transit the wild safely.

In this regard, we are now prepared to understand fully human *value* as wealth was intended to be judged. Such wealth is not acquired through accumulation, but through appreciation and consideration. A wealthy individual, say, is not someone who merely owns a great many automobiles, but someone who may own a great many *types* of automobiles. The collector versus the consumer, in other words. The one who appreciates versus the one who merely accumulates.

From this context, we can begin to understand human value itself. A value both extraordinarily unique and simplistically similar. First, the human being remains valuable for simply being a human *person* – all men created equal. Secondly, being human – rather than, say, an ostrich – people bear *potential* that other species do not possess. We can both accumulate wealth *and* appreciate it. Or, perhaps more politely, we can achieve success *and* use that success to benefit others as well as ourselves.

A squirrel may accumulate nuts, and perhaps even appreciate its winter's store insofar as rodents can appreciate such things, but these small animals do not feel morally obligated to dispense these stores amongst the less fortunate squirrel herd. Yet, people *do* share and contribute, strive and cajole, demand and earn. These represent desires that exceed beyond the pure need to survive (sharing can be deadly during a famine, for instance).

These characteristics increase human value infinitely – particularly for those one billion or more Christians around the world who believe that God Himself came to earth, to share in our humanity, and to die upon the Cross, for our sins. This divine fusion with humans propels Western civilization ahead the rest of the world in such decidedly human concepts as forgiveness, charity, and, most especially, *freedom.*

The concept of freedom itself bears scrutiny for our discussion. Here, we are less inclined towards libertarian or licentiousness views. Rather, we are talking primarily about *free will.* That *all* people were granted certain "inalienable rights" from their Creator, as defined within the U.S. Declaration of Independence, yet that people bore a tremendous responsibility to behave ethically lest they (in Christian terms) be punished in hell.

In discussing freedom, we can shorten the concept to attributes most familiar – and expected by – civilized peoples. These are, of course, the freedom to think and to learn, the freedom to worship God as we so choose, and the freedom to live our lives as we see fit. As human individuals, however, we cannot keep our beliefs and lives buried underneath a bushel basket. To think and to learn matters little unless we can travel amongst others and teach. To worship God matters little unless we can do so openly with others and without fear of reprisal, even if we are in a public square. To live as we see fit matters little unless we can do so without undue fear that *others'* living does not place us into direct harm.

Because human individuals corral much more of the spiritual world – again, North American squirrels cannot care about, say, Asian bears – our inherent value rests far beyond our mere bodies. After all, we remain the *only* species thus far to invent rock and roll music and stoplight drag races. We also understand calculus, nuclear physics, and the human genome. Yet, none of this knowledge – as humanly great as it is – defines us specifically as anything other than *Homo sapiens*. We are much more than warm-blooded creatures with a large brain and opposable digits.

Human beings remain a social creature, which means that our happiness rests with companionship, communication, and compassion. We weep whenever we see a small child injured. Our hearts sadden whenever we learn of an elderly person that has died. We leap to our feet when our sports team wins and collapse to our knees when a natural disaster hits a city on the far end of the country. These are *shared* qualities, things that educate (and explain to) us about the collective human family that is ours to behold.

Nevertheless, there remain others – a comparably small population, but present just the same – who do not share in this human concept of socialization. Some of these individuals simply do not believe in the presence of human freedom. They believe that individuals are not sufficiently educated or, perhaps, experienced enough to influence the world without (usually) governmental guidance. Another group cares even less about humanity. They simply believe in self-deification, to a degree, and expect others to kowtow to his or her whims and if we do not, then they will kill us without as much as a second thought.

This latter group will kill simply for the sake of killing, although such actions may frequent any number of "justifications" within his or her mind. Adolf Hitler's Nazis, for instance, hated Jews whom they blamed for post-First World War Germany's economic crises and failures during the conflict. Jeffrey Dahmer raped, murdered, dissected, and *ate* innocent men and boys over a thirteen-year period ending in 1991.

These two examples prove that some individuals

can be as barbaric as humanly possible and that whether acting alone or in groups, they decide who lives and who dies. We can only do whatever it takes to stop them before they attack for their legions are too numerous to eradicate completely. Nor are their methods, which range from bombs to guns to poisons and just about every other natural and artificial cause of death.

3. SURVIVAL

WITHIN the deepest recesses of the human mind lurks the primal force evolved for personal survival. This represents the process by which we are born literally kicking and screaming; having been thrust into an alien environment for which we have *never* experienced before that period, an infant cries in terror until it can sense the warmth and love of its mother.

Once the human mind matured to the point where it observed other human persons, it resorted to another layer – the competitive or aggressive phase. Herein the individual challenged all newcomers for the best caves in which to live, the best food sources, and, obviously, the best women with which to father children. Next up the evolutionary scale, human thought processes determined that *some* things were worth bargaining for or sharing with those who held more. This indicates an alliance-building or cooperative phase that increased the holdings of small groups or clans.

As needs further grew along with the population, the ever-innovative human mind conceived of society building, a process by which larger groups of all sizes developed and codified "proper" behavior and expectations for the betterment of that culture. Individuals were selected for leadership positions and everyone found what his best talent was in order to contribute towards that great society of theirs. Within this environment, some worked hard and others not nearly so, some developed new innovations while others had to learn, many fought with one another while still others served as peacekeepers.

This ultimately leads to the final phase of mental development for humanity – the discovery of entitlements. Here is where individuals learned to seek *specific* goals that he or she believed that they deserved regardless of external influence. One person, for example, decided that he would only hunt certain foods and not grow crops. Another, perhaps, sought to cease working as soon as the sun set while his neighbor may have decided not to work at all once the rains came pouring down.

The ultimate – and fully expected – conclusion of the human mental process rests with the entitlement to become lackadaisical, spontaneous, and carefree about life. In its most apparent form, this involves such diverse examples as people retiring at a certain age, more often than not at a fixed pension, universal healthcare, and the abandonment for a need to *fight* to survive. In this latter regard, we have assumed that *others* would do the dirty work; all that we require is to cry "wolf!" and the sheepdogs would come running to our – and our *exclusive* – aid.

Unfortunately, as soon as others discovered this easy life, more people joined the ranks and by our 21st century, there remain simply not enough "sheepdogs" to come to our assistance whether our house is on fire or an attacker is assailing us. The ultimate course of human development seems to parrot "Let someone *else* do it!"

When, precisely, we allowed our safety and

survival to be placed upon the shoulders of others is not readily known. It may have begun when monarchies decided that families and friends were insufficient to defend the crown, so the kings and queens decided that actually *paying* soldiers represented a better way to protect. Perhaps, it was when public educational systems developed and, as students, we were no longer required to explore and learn on our own. Now, all we had to do was chose a subject and expect someone else to convert us from neophyte into scholar.

As civilization increased, we became weaker and woefully inadequate to adjust to major changes. This is evident in the way that we riot and loot during crises quicker than we come together to help. As people, we are simply *entitled* to steal rather than assist. At least that is how a publicly sizeable portion of the population seems to believe. Since most people retreat to their homes during such crises, all that the world observes on television remains the malcontents looting and burning their cities down.

For society as a whole, this is deeply disturbing. The message sent is that during any form of disturbance, the vast majority of law-abiding citizens will stay at home effectively turning their communities over to hordes of thugs and limited police presence. And when the fires finally die down, it remains the villains who cry foul over the use of such terms as "thugs" while others quickly blame the police for any transgressions. Further complicating the matter remains as populations increase, taxpayer-funded police agencies will dwindle as off-balanced economies prevent cities from providing for protection as politicians seek to patronize entitlement-demanding citizens.

At this point, the concerned individual must realize that not all is hopeless. Despite the presence of so many uncaring looters and malcontents, safety is in the hands of the threatened individual. As long as he or she does not *panic* and reacts according to preconditioned responses, even relatively untrained individuals can sneak out of adversarial confrontations. The key rests upon a key element known to *anyone* who has ever endured military basic training.

The common misconception amongst the population is that a person "rises to the occasion" during any crisis. This could not be further from the truth. In reality, as is known to all military personnel, people fall back upon their *lowest level of training*, which is why military 'boot camp' is designed to shatter the parental upbringing of soldiers and sailors. Militaries, primarily those of Western democracies, condition their members to respond to varying crises *subconsciously* in order to deal with the matter before pampered human conditioning takes over.

This is also why martial artists engage within dedicated drills prior to breaking boards or blocks with his or her head. Any rational individual would believe that they would crush their skull or hand rather than the targeted board. And they would because the subconscious human condition is to *cease* striking at the target because of this aforementioned thought and *this* leads to injury – not the actual breaking of the board itself. Just ask any ill-tempered individual who has punched a hole into the wall during a fit of rage.

Survival, thus, represents a two-way street. On the one hand, it riles our temperament so that we remain capable of shattering an attacker's nose should they assault us. On the other hand, however, it keeps us from trying this routine too many times less we break our own hand instead of the object that we are focusing upon. This represents a healthy balance, except that modern humans have shifted the delicate equation towards hesitance.

So powerful is this wavering behavior that even our elected and appointed officials believe that subjugation remains best for us. This is why they tell us to "give your possessions to the robber, your life is far more valuable than your wallet or your purse." Of course, human lives are far more valuable than material possessions, which is why human lives should be protected *at all costs*. Simply allowing thieves and others to attack humans – psychologically or physically – unmolested *diminishes* the value of that human individual.

Remember, as we have already discussed, the most basic of human thoughts rests with fighting others for food and shelter. In this regard, our primal human nature rests with *punishing* – not supporting – those who wish to take things away from us. Eons ago, if we freely gave away food we would have starved to death. Today, we would both starve and drop ourselves into a stupor from which never to recover.

A long, healthy life is a form of personal wealth and success. To achieve it, requires the same five elements as financial fortune. Further, we must be resilient and disciplined in our manner of affecting it. We also need skill (knowledge) and common sense. Most importantly, however, we need the *desire* to survive and this requires a great deal of effort on our part. As with all thinks in life, the strongest and best trained succeed the most.

When it comes to *organized* crime – drug traffickers, terrorists, anarchists, etc. – individuals must join like-minded groups in order to bear an equal footing. This means that *communities* must organize against dispersed threats. The primary reason for this, of course, rests with the inability of municipal authorities adequately to protect communities at large and isolated segments of that society in particular. Every major Western nation now possesses segments of that society, mostly in larger cities but not necessarily exclusively, where police officers fear to go into. These represent "ungoverned spaces" located in the heart of supposedly *governed* municipalities.

If any of this appears troubling to you, then you hear the faint declarations of your distant ancestors suggesting that it remains no hallmark of civilization to cast the deepest recesses of your human psychology into the carelessly run halls of to whichever bureaucracy you belong. Institutions, particularly those led by transitory politicians, will *never* care about your personal survival for halfway through their term, they remain as likely to adjust to personal agendas required by election cycles than govern the way that he or she was elected to abide by.

There is a strong lesson from one famous case study. At 12 years old, actor Bruce Lee was accosted and beaten up by a street gang. This inspired the young Lee to take up martial arts and with only about five years' professional training, went on to become *the* icon of modern martial arts and singlehandedly led to the rise of "karate flicks". Known for his two-finger pushups, Lee proved that *anyone* could achieve extraordinary achievements in the field of survival if he or she simply possessed the drive to succeed.

This effort must relinquish the traditional modern view that individualism – in its less obstructive definition – is dangerous to society.

Bureaucrats remain your most determined enemy, for personal defense (a requisite for survival) requires their support through endless regulations, legislation, and whatever tax they can charge you and get away with. Nevertheless, your human psyche pushes you to survive despite the pressures of conformity.

You struggle to work each day that you are sick, not because you fear losing your job, but because you understand that losing your job seriously affects your ability to survive. You cram for those final exams not because you want to boast about your mental capacity, but subconsciously you fear *failing* the exams and, therefore, your survival through school may end abruptly or extended. *Everything* that you do rests upon survival – failure or success.

Much the same exists with rooting for your favorite sports team. Whether or not your favorite team wins the championship will not affect your life, but losing it does make you believe that life will be unbearable – if only for the briefest of moments – should you encounter your friends that supported the winning side. Surviving *is* being human.

If this were not the case, then you would not observe, for instance, rabid anti-gun people declaring all manners of outrage over the mere sight of a firearm. The gun in and of itself is not threatening; at least there are no known firearms walking around on artificial legs seeking to shoot humans without human input. Rather, the *presence* of that firearm sends chills up these individuals' spine. *Why?*

First, they express a fundamental ignorance over the function and use of firearms. Second, they fear that the existence within the hands of the population threatens his or her political and social beliefs. Both of these statements rest upon survival –

one personal and the other professional. It is that they try to prevent *your survival* that makes his or her beliefs tyrannical.

Because survival represents the foundational precept of the human mind, it presumes that such survival transcends both political and personal opinion. That is, when survival becomes deeply critical, such as during a riot or war, it is very likely that *governing authority* will have simply vanished. At least temporarily. To place contextual or measured restrictions on survival is absurd. *Every* human individual bears the right to defend him or herself against harm – providing that such defense does not indiscriminately harm other innocent souls.

4. DEFENSE

THE *Catechism of the Catholic Church*[1] offers several statements regarding the act of self-defense that we must consider in any communal discussion on the act of using violence – emotional intensity of action – to effect survival. Let us consider the Roman Catholic view of self-defense:

♦ "The legitimate defense of persons and societies is not an exception to the prohibition against the murder of the innocent that constitutes intentional killing. 'The act of self-defense can have a double effect: the preservation of one's own life; and the killing of the aggressor..The one is intended, the other is not.'" (#2263)

♦ "Love toward oneself remains a fundamental principal of morality. Therefore it is legitimate to insist on respect for one's own right to life. Someone who defends his life is not guilty of murder even if he is forced to deal his aggressor a lethal blow: If a man in self-defense uses more than necessary violence, it will be unlawful:

---

[1] United States Catholic Conference, Inc., *Catechism of the Catholic Church* (New York: Doubleday, 1994), Specific passages given in parentheses (Paragraph Number).

whereas if he repels force with moderation, his defense will be lawful....Nor is it necessary for salvation that a man omit the act of moderate self-defense to avoid killing the other man, since one is bound to take more care of one's own life than of another's." (#2264)

♦ "Legitimate defense can be not only a right but a grave duty for someone responsible for another's life, the common good of the family or of the state." (#2265).

♦ "Preserving the common good of society requires rendering the aggressor unable to inflict harm. For this reason the traditional teaching of the Church has acknowledged as well-founded the right and duty of legitimate public authority to punish malefactors by means of penalties commensurate with the gravity of the crime, not excluding, in cases of extreme gravity, the death penalty. For analogous reasons those holding authority have the right to repel by armed force aggressors against the community in their charge." (#2266)

These four paragraphs grant both individuals and communities the expressed right to defend themselves against aggression – armed or otherwise. We only need to touch upon a few phrases to authenticate *armed* defense against aggressors.

First, and most importantly, we consent that it remains a "grave duty" to defend oneself, his or her family, and any community of individuals. Second, we declare that it remains quite legitimate to insist upon our own right to life. That is, "...since one is bound to take more care of one's own life than of another's." Third, the preservation of society requires that individuals within that society render aggressors unable to inflict harm. Finally, those with *authority* – though not expressly elected or appointed authority – "have the right to repel by armed force" anyone attacking his or her community.

This does *not* mean that individuals bear a right to go around shooting up the environment – that is the role of an aggressor. Yet it *does* mean that individuals and communities of individuals bear the right to use whatever means may be necessary to render that aggressor unable to inflict harm and firearms remain the most viable option in most circumstances (their remaining compact, relatively inexpensive and available, and most people can learn to use one responsibly with minimal training and practice).

The key consideration in our discussion is that individuals remain more valuable than the collective does and that "authority" need not represent bureaucratic politicians or distant police officers. After all, defense is required *at the scene* and not outside any perimeter. Writing about the seemingly ubiquitous case of school shootings, author and military researcher H. John Poole states that the vast majority of people would not want police officers "carefully marshalling one's forces outside the school to insure proper coordination between elements", rather that he or she prefers "immediately sending two highly trained officers into the school to confront the killer."[2]

More likely, however, the average citizen – regardless of country – would prefer at least two highly trained personnel *already existing* within the school to

---

[2] H. John Poole, *Tequila Junction: 4ᵗʰ-Generation Counterinsurgency*

take down perpetrators of terror. We shall discuss this in detail later on within this book. For the moment, we need to focus upon the act of defense itself and our moral obligations to affect it.

Although we each bear a fundamental right to life – in the words of the aforementioned *Catechism*: "The inalienable right to life of every innocent human individual is a *constitutive element of a civil society and its legislation*"[3] – people are not guaranteed of "safety". This latter statement presupposes a great deal of responsibility on the part of the individual. To remain safe, we must live life responsibly, pay close attention to threatening situations and people, and act according to our intellect and conscience.

Naturally, people participating in such activities as extreme sports must not expect that our society will cover their every whim should they receive injuries within their chosen leisure profession. Nor can such others within what one author calls our "danger loving society" expect that society, as a whole to bail out their families should he or she die within the activity.[4] As with survival, relative safety requires effort upon the part of the individual.

In this regard, we cannot relinquish our natural right to life to those parties whose legislation and/or affiliations may not agree with our safety. In other words, survival is what *you* make of it because few others are going to accord you due diligence when it comes to, say, saving your particular life over another's. That is, people tend to become rather selfish

---

(Emerald Isle, NC: Posterity Press, 2008), `82.
[3] *Catechism*, #2273
[4] David A. Grossman, "Defeating the Enemy's Will: The Psychological Foundations of Maneuver Warfare" in *Maneuver Warfare: An Anthology*, ed. Richard D. Hooker, Jr. (Novato, CA: Presidio Press, 1993), 151-153.

when both your lives are at risk.

Nevertheless, there remain periods in which it may behoove you to care about others – such as when the passengers of United Airlines Flight 93 rose up in near unison to defeat the fourth hijacked aircraft on September 11, 2001. Environmental conditions, such as your presence within a shopping mail or movie theater, for instance, mandate that you combine your efforts with others to shore your individual safety. This represents the basis for "community security" and the situation encompasses one of the following:

- ✓ Your presence within the environment is restricted by congestion and safe egress requires the participation of at least a portion of the population that blocks your route to safety.

- ✓ Individuals under your care exist within that particular environment and simply protecting yourself is not a satisfactory option (such as when your children sit within a particular classroom or you represent the teacher whose function is to protect all individuals within your area of influence).

- ✓ Areas within your community face internal and external threats that may compromise your business, your employer, your source of food and water, or your safe transit into and out of that location.

- ✓ Events outside your community force large groups of others to flee chaos and migrate towards your otherwise peaceful location.

These conditions, particularly the last two, prevent

self-reliance upon security for others within the immediate area preclude individual action.

At a minimum, your actions for self-defense will require securing "non-aggression" pacts with your immediate neighbors. In other words, you have to keep your neighbors involved lest they thwart your protection – intentionally or unintentionally. Unless you remain alone and confronting a mugger in a parking garage, for example, the odds remain exceedingly rare that you will *not* involve a multitude of other individuals – even if you merely cry out for assistance. Therefore, it is better to involve others from the start.

Community security is also the most accepted form of defense, for the inclusion of others speaks of tolerance and conference, which further ensures that "loose cannons" do not roll around destroying the best-laid plans. Communities also benefit from competitive adaptation, which means that individuals with divergent experiences and knowledge can contribute in order to make the whole greater than the sum of its parts. Narcotics traffickers, for instance, often share equipment and tactics, engaging within "brainstorming sessions" to ensure that the best approach to defeating law enforcement is utilized. Would it not be beneficial for communities to do the same in the war against such criminals?

Furthermore, this sharing of effort ensures that the community as a whole develops its own persona of resolve: less qualified and less motivated individuals will be taught and inspired by those with greater personal abilities. In fact, *inspiration* may be the greatest asset of the community; the fundamental threat to survival representing isolation and fear.

The first step, however, remains to take stock of

your community's resources, threat assessments, and expected participation. Such analysis may approximate the following considerations:

- *Emerging threats.* Communities not only face *present* threats, they confront future threats too. For instance, if a major petroleum structure were routed through your community, then you can anticipate an increase in crime across the board. Similarly, if you were to gain a new sports stadium or entertainment complex. Any new development that offers economic profit and employment will necessarily draw in criminals seeking to capitalize upon "easy money" and, perhaps, terrorists seeking to send messages throughout the world. In most Western nations, narcotic traffickers have encroached upon nearly every urban center that promises a steady supply of addicted citizens.

- *Personnel.* Regardless of the size of any one particular community, it offers a wealth of diversity and ingenuity within its residents. Nevertheless, not all of these citizens are properly motivated or will come to the aid of others, necessitating that that community's leaders need to become versed in human resources (there is likely to be a skilled HR representative within your town or city).These potential recruits should be classified into such categories as creative personality versus analytical personality, "big picture" thinkers versus "small picture" thinkers, and so on. Each individual must be placed according to his or her talents, education, and experience without unnecessary regard to longevity or seniority (as would be the case, say, with active military and labor unions).

- *Resources.* With a fully developed community security force in mind, what, precisely, are your equipment expectations? Will you simply be a walkabout group intended as good Samaritans destined to play adult boy scouts like the Guardian Angels? Or were you dreaming of an armed paramilitary force or militia that eagerly awaits for the day when society will collapse and you shall take full advantage of the situation? Frankly, your options are limited by national and local laws. Simply walking down the public sidewalk bearing a dust broom may even be considered as "armed and dangerous" in public. That said, you must make maximum use of what remains permissible within your particular community.

- *Limitations and liabilities.* This represents probably the most overlooked portion of community security arrangements. *Whatever* you do to protect your local community, one thing that we *can* guarantee is that you will ultimately be sued or challenged regarding your efforts. Citizens attending courses to receive a concealed carry permit to bear a pistol understand this intimately; if *anyone* defends his or her life, regardless of whether they were attacked or not, his or her life will be *irreparably harmed.* Likely, he or she will face years' worth of court challenges (from the aggressor's next of kin, naturally) and psychological distress. The same holds true for your family. If you were, say, to stop an active shooter, then your community will be on the television news for weeks and the repercussions will last for decades in newspapers and textbooks. And, very likely, *not* for saving human lives.

These considerations will aid in fermenting a community-wide security defense program, but they do not reprcscnt the *only* contingencies. Much effort lies ahead once the local leaders assess the threats, people, resources, and limitations they are confronted with.

As with the physical world through which we pass, every action taken produces an opposite reaction, which, in our case, may not necessarily be equal in force. For instance, announce to the public that you are developing community security and your offices will be flooded with a range of people, some heralding your efforts and some trying to sabotage them. A vast majority, however, may likely question the sincerity or intent of your mission.

For this reason, community defense plans should be restricted to specific sub-communities of your town or city. That is, arrangements made for schools and universities or churches and clinics, for example, offer better opportunities to skirt the feedback. Here is where defenders find the right mix of defined territories, screened employees, and public expectations for safety.

Each of these sample locations also represent "soft targets", which means that *any* attempt to shore up their defenses will improve public safety exponentially. We will discuss these individual needs and opportunities within the appropriate chapter of this book, but for the moment, we have yet to define clearly *how* we should defend our lives. As with everything in life, our objective rests with the building blocks that will permit us to achieve that final construction: community security.

We have learned, for analogy, that survival remains the foundation upon which we plan our structure, regardless of how high or mighty we seek it to be. Defense, for its role, represents the framework that will hold the edifice together and keep it from collapsing down upon itself. With an attitude of survival and a clear ambition for defense, individuals and communities stand a greater chance for survival. However, neither a solid foundation nor a strong framework will arise without proper architecture and regulation. Herein is where your security plan takes shape in order to guide your future "construction".

5. MARTIAL TACTICS

VICTORY requires obsession. The obsession to succeed despite the challenges and setbacks one faces. A professional athlete, for instance, must learn how to cope with injury, fatigue, insult, and competition just to participate within his or her chosen sport. To win an actual championship, however, requires a great deal more. Michael Jordan, for one, practiced free throws all day long while his school friends wanted to go out and enjoy themselves. Professional hockey players routinely tell stories about how their parents drove them to practice during the early morning hours before heading out to school and work, respectively.

Yet, had any of these athletes failed in his or her endeavors, it would not represent the end of life for them, as would failure to survive for you. Their particular obsession was, beyond all doubt, his or her life's passion. They succeeded because they exercised acute *discipline* to ensure that his or her obsessive devotion to task had guidance and resilience. In other words, they bore a *tactical plan* of action that nearly always stood from childhood onwards.

Unfortunately, your particular situation probably means that you represent a relative novice when it comes to matters of security. There is nothing inherently wrong with this; rather, that you must work even harder to catch up to speed with your more professional peers. Of course, your relative innocence means that you will not fall for traditional thinking as you begin to learn and question everything that appears "strange" to you. You are unlikely to be attracted to expensive, complicated technologies and bureaucratic strategies.

What you *cannot* skimp on, however, rests with the actual tactical plan that serves as the guidebook for your unique community. Think of this as similar to a musical score sheet. Your community shares an overall idea of what it wants to achieve, but with each individual offering a different "instrument" to play, you must possess a symphonic agreement otherwise harmony collapses into noise rather than music. Criminals target that particular "noise" because it represents disorganization and vulnerability.

Your ultimate goal represents a solid plan that, while uncomplicated and virtually unseen, still promotes the image of unity of purpose for would-be aggressors. And they *will* be able to notice the difference between, say, a school managed chaotically from one whose staff keeps on their toes. The mere presence of professionalism speaks louder than words and, even at worst, criminals will *suspect* an actionable security plan at work even if they cannot decipher one through school bulletins and parental guidebooks (and they *do* read such publications).

The first step for you is to identify what your community represents. Is it an elementary or secondary school? A small college or major university? An office suite or a towering building? Whatever your situation, large or small, your plan must build upon the smallest defensible space and work outwards from there. If yours were a small school, for example, then you would undoubtedly build your tactical security plan around individual classrooms. Conversely, if your environment represented a large industrial complex, you may not be able to secure voluminous production floors with their complex equipment. Therefore, passageways and outlying buildings – readily accessible through securable corridors, of course – would be your primary consideration.

Before we continue, we should remind the reader of several important considerations to keep in mind when planning your community's safe zones:

1. Moving targets are harder to strike.

2. Expanding groups make direction harder to decipher (e.g., is this mass of people moving towards me or away?).

3. A single attacker *cannot* target more than one person at a time.

4. People habitually look *down* rather than up.

5. Attackers enter a community with preconceived notions of what he or she is likely to face.

These five statements will make planning your tactical actions simpler, but they will *not* eliminate threats. What is required remains to fuse these considerations into your particular environment and employ them to evaluate what could be accomplished within your unique scenario.

For example, when confronted with an active shooter in a school, the *last* thing that you want is for twenty or thirty students to bunker down within an accessible classroom. Your students' best chances for survival, in that case, are to disperse them as widely and as quickly as possible. If this shooter is bearing a handgun, then he or she is unlikely to have more than 15 shots available before reloading, depending upon the type and design of the firearm. If a rifle, then that figure tops out at about thirty rounds on average.

Despite media hysterics involving high-capacity magazines and, perhaps, multiple firearms, it still takes a few seconds in order to swap out magazines or change firearms. Mere seconds, of course, but football, basketball, and hockey teams often win games with only those seemingly brief seconds left. You may as well...keep those students running into different (but preplanned and well-rehearsed!) directions and even non-athletes can cover twenty-two feet per second in a run (or 15 m.p.h., slightly more than thrice as fast as the average person can walk).

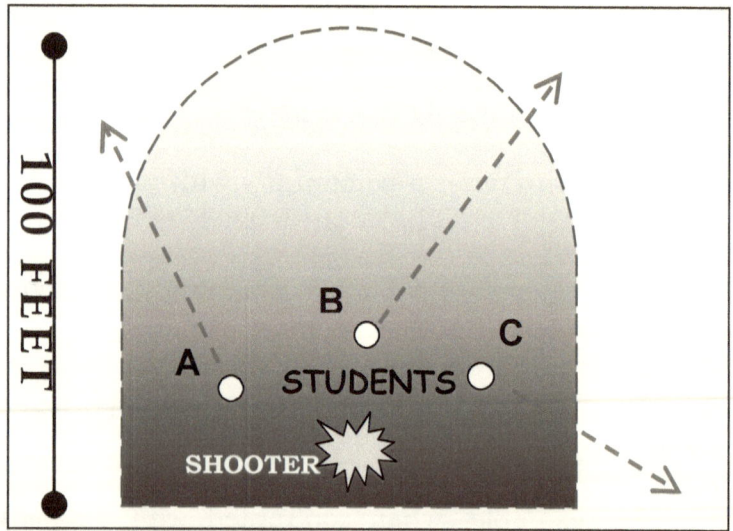

Figure 1. Effective range of an average shooter.

If we examine Figure 1, we observe a brief scenario in which an active shooter is targeting three students over a period of three seconds. The effective range (as depicted) of an average shooter, targeting moving objects while under duress (only the "emotionless" shooters remain calm), is about 100 feet (~ 30 meters). Although many environment considerations such as elevation, obstacles, etc. must be considered, this illustration shows, in the simplest terms, how *dispersion* may affect the outcome of an active shooter situation.

All three students remain within the shooter's most effective range at the start, but emerge from the gunman's most effective range within about three seconds. Note, the shooter's effective range is more intense, but shorter towards the left and right. This is because as a shooter pivots to either side, he or she tends to focus upon those targets closer in to his or her person. This is a natural human reaction as people tend to be momentarily "dazed" during quick turns and therefore the brain is hardwired to retreat to its *survival mode* before it can consider threats that may be more distant. In this case, Student C has to run the least distance for effective escape.

Student B, standing directly in front of the aggressor, has to run the greatest distance because, although he or she is running towards the left, they remain within the shooter's focus for the longest period. Student A, in the peripheral, has decided to assume lesser of an angle away from the shooter's vision.

Again, many factors not depicted affect this scenario, but the illustration serves to visualize the concept of dispersal. Even with only three victims present, a shooter would have to pivot wildly to target all of them, leading to drastically reduced efficiency. The key to consider is that criminals, even hardened "street tough" ones, generally do *not* expect to be attacked themselves or observe evasive maneuvers. This merely adds to the effectiveness of those precious few seconds that dispersal aids.

In planning your community's tactical plan for survival, you must include both active measures as well as passive approaches to security. The above illustration suggests an *active* measure, but its implementation must be passive – training students and other bystanders to *act* rather than react to crises well beforehand. Upon first sighting of an armed intruder or the hearing of the first few shots of a firearm, he or she must *instinctively* go into dispersion mode.

Active and passive measures may take the following examples:

Active Measures:

- Employing armed personnel – professionals or trained staff – to confront suspicious persons.

- Security barriers preventing easy access yet permitting rapid egress from the facility or compound.

- Active denial systems – sound or heat sources that disrupt an aggressor's ability to concentrate or move into certain areas.

- Barricading innocent persons within rooms with whatever equipment or supplies may be available.

- Employing improvised weaponry to attack aggressors.

Passive Measures.

- Scheduling classes or shifts at differing times to prevent outsiders from gaining awareness of personnel movements.

- Clandestine paths of egress and evasion known only to students, employees, patients, etc.

- Researching previous incidents to evaluate their potential for your particular environment.

- Attending security-related courses and seminars.

- Hiring consultants to "red team" (i.e., function as adversaries) various scenarios.

- Develop strong working relationships with local authorities.

You will note from the above that even "passive" security measures require a fair amount of effort on your part and that of your community.

Your tactical plan, itself, requires extraordinary attention to detail and, more importantly, forethought. Your particular community does not want to be forced to come up with plans *when* an aggressor actually shows up at your establishment, but that itself always remains a probability because innovative threats always try to find your Achilles' heel.

You may also find yourself more comfortable with passive approaches than active ones. For instance, if your school or company resides, regrettably, within a location that restricts firearms possession, then you may have no other recourse than to accept a passive slant towards security. Similarly, guards walking around toting assault rifles at a church may prevent parishioners from attending services for fear that "something" may have gone wrong. Or else, they may simply feel ill at ease, for instance, praying a rosary if such guards are walking around as if in combat.

Naturally, students at a public school may not fully appreciate "freedom" if they feel as if studying at a penitentiary or military compound. On the other hand, citizens just *may* feel a bit more relieved if they observe such activities at airports, sporting events, or shopping malls as most people today have heard about suicide bombings and terrorist attacks at such places. The tactical perspective remains just that, a *perspective*.

Your community must walk the fine line between not offending those under your care and offending those who would try to harm those under your care. The first you do not wish to antagonize and the second you must make all efforts to "render unable to inflict harm". At least, you want to make potential criminals flee or capitulate based primarily upon your active and passive "posturing" program.

In effect, your tactical plan outline should look something like the following example. What you contain within this document will be covered within subsequent chapters. For the moment, use it to consider how such a plan *might* look from your perspective. You will need to be creative and improvisational, practical and resourceful, realistic and subjective. To survive, you cannot rely *solely* upon others to author your security doctrine, for only those things that *you* place effort into are likely to be utilized by your particular community. Make the plan *your* passion.

SECURITY PLAN FOR ANYTOWN SCHOOL
Approved by Frank Superintendent

TABLE OF CONTENTS

1. Background
2. Introduction
3. Personnel Disposition and Responsibilities.
4. Procedures
  - Fires
  -Weather disturbances
  -Active shooters
  -Terrorism
5. Physical Measures.
6. Training
7. Supplemental data

Frank Superintendent   *Joe Teacher*
Modified by   Received by

SEAL

Figure 2. Sample school tactical plan outline.

In Figure 2 we see a sample tactical plan outline for a small school, which we have located within Anytown, U.S.A. This document should be contained within a loose-leaf folder so that pages may be removed and others added as situations warrant. Note, however, that *each page* of the plan must contain provisions for signatories to modify and receive each individual page (perhaps signing major sections and then only initialing the page additions). This is done, obviously, to ensure that all school staff have read and endorsed the measures, be they original or new in publication. Failure often rests upon "I did not know *that*!" or "I never *saw* that change!" Make certain that *everyone* does know or see such important documents.

With the sample outline in Figure 2 in mind, we can discuss what might be contained within each section, permitting the reader to adjust the requisite data for his or her unique environment whether that is a school, church, industrial institution, or hospital. With our brief examples, on these pages and within subsequent chapters, you should be able to anticipate your particular requirements and build a personal plan from these thoughts and future research.

Let us, therefore, begin with the very basics:

BACKGROUND

Before one even begins to introduce a tactical plan for others to follow, it is best to remind him or her of *why*, precisely, there exists such a plan. If your community represents a school, then you may discuss active shooters, suicide bombers, narcotics dealers, disgruntled stepparents, child custody cases, etc. that appear within the news or have taken place in the past. If yours represents an industrial plant, conversely, then you would want to include subjects such as espionage, environmental activism, labor disputes, domestic violence (belligerent ex-spouses, etc.), disgruntled employees, etc.

Whatever your particular community represents, you *must* outline to your staff that the days of leaving doors unlocked and permitting unofficial visitors has disappeared. Anyone and *anything* can be considered a viable threat today. You must use current and historical information to show that such things not only happen, but they occur much closer to home with each passing year. A simple discussion of technology and globalization along with a healthy dose of personal research should provide your staff with enough information to shatter any preconceived notions of "peace". Furthermore, such activities contribute towards your own evolution as community leader.

INTRODUCTION

Once you have set the stage, so to speak, you must write an introductory section that personifies the above information with your particular situation in mind. You must address the unique nature of your community and the vulnerabilities that it exhibits. For instance, you may state that your church suffers from too many people glued to the altar, wherein there may not be enough ushers on staff to confront people that "sneak" up behind your congregation. Alternately, if your community represents a hospital, you may write about the growing number of incidences where nurses have been attacked or addicted persons have sought a "free" supply of drugs.

The Introduction Section takes "what is happening" around the world and explains why *your* community may be next in line to be attacked. For example, if you remain responsible for a synagogue, *any* activity involving the Israeli-Arab situation will undoubtedly make your community a target for anti-Semitic individuals and groups that cannot – or will not – travel overseas to "join the fight" as it were. Alternatively, as a school, you may introduce that the

May 18, 1927 Bath, Michigan disaster resulted from a resident's (and former school board treasurer) hatred of paying taxes for the new school, which coincided with his loss of farm through tax foreclosure[5]; a similar situation with your community may create comparable issues. At a minimum, your school will realize that school massacres are *not* necessarily new or even gun-related.

PERSONNEL DISPOSITION AND RESPONSIBILITIES

With the prerequisites out of the way, you will now be in a better position to analyze your staff and volunteers and place them into positions of importance regarding community security. Herein you shift your priorities from the subjective to the objective and from the observant to the participatory. Every person within your organization will serve a *specific* – and due to a scarcity of both personnel and resources – and extremely critical function.

Depending upon the size and nature of your facility or community, you will need the following roles filled:

Security Coordinator. This individual will serve as your community's primary 'go to' person regarding security. He or she will conduct the necessary research and investigation into *your* primary needs and place into effect whatever security provisions your community requires, including the implementation of

---

[5] For additional information on this singularly disastrous attack, visit http://freepages.history.rootsweb.ancestry.com/~bauerle/disaster.htm and http://www.findagrave.com/cgi-bin/fg.cgi?page=gr&GSvcid=4972&GRid=7856467&, both accessed October 2015.

scheduling, authorization procedures, and authentication of any alterations thereof.

Training Director. Security rests upon training, therefore your community will need someone that can place ideas into motion and ensure that all participants receive the proper training, attend any requisite seminars, and make certain that your tactical plan involves personnel that can actually do the job. This job is part researcher, part inspirational coach, and part career counselor all rolled into one neat package.

Firearms Specialist. If any of your people carry firearms as part of his or her primary function (less if they carry personally as part of a state-licensed concealed weapons program), you will need a firearms specialist or armorer who can keep abreast of the latest developments within this field. Such a person will intimately understand the nature of ammunition within your environment (say, the use of frangible bullets that will not over-penetrate doors and walls), which firearms offer the most effective function within your facility and outlying buildings, and ensure that all staff – including those not necessarily carrying firearms – remain trained in their use (e.g., a non-armed teacher may have to recover the firearm of a wounded comrade in order to save others, etc.).

Architectural Specialist. This position studies and observes the field known as Crime Prevention through Environmental Design, or CPTED. Briefly, this discipline works to reduce crime through *how* a particular building or compound is designed and constructed. For instance, well lit parking lots, parking garages with few solid barriers (which shield crimes underway), and heavy thorn bushes near windows (which prohibit less motivated thieves from breaking in), are all practices developed by CPTED. As most businesses, schools, churches, and hospitals eventually grow in size, these personnel retain his or her usefulness to any farsighted community.

Information Technologist.   Any organization that utilizes computers requires someone versed in hardware, software, Web presence, and social media. This person may handle these functions as part of his or her ordinary position, but when it comes to security, they cannot be diverted away from ensuring the safety of your community's data and its members' personal information. Criminals and terrorists of all persuasions remain experts in targeting organizations through the manipulation of data, blackmail (present Russian gangs are "locking down" computers of innocent parties and then blackmailing them into large sums of money just to "release" the use of his or her computer), and pre-attack rehearsing.

Other positions to be considered. Very large institutions and communities may require a hazardous materials technician, decontamination specialist, and a counter-threat finance manager amongst other specialized technicians.

PROCEDURES

When a crisis happens, whether it remains as relatively innocuous as a small fire or as devastating as an active shooter incident, your community's actions in response to the event will determine whether you emerge from the challenge with minimal or significant damage. This is difficult for the simple reason that if you knew what was going to happen beforehand, then you would obviously suffer minimal – if any – problems. The truth is, the worst things happen when we cannot possibly perceive them (think of the September 11, 2001 attacks, for example).

You will need procedures in place to handle the most diverse of crises and, yet, you will still be caught facing something fully unexpected. For instance, tragically, school massacres appear rather commonplace today and are incorporated into any school or university's contingency plans. Yet, no one could have foreseen Andrew Kehoe's blowing up the school in Bath, Michigan back on May 18, 1927. Such things were inconceivable back then. What might *your* community experience that appears just as unfathomable today?

One only has to watch a cable television news channel for a day to realize that horrible things happen quite frequently. Much is made of the Islamic State in Iraq and Syria (ISIS) beheading innocent people or burning them alive for propaganda value. However, *Los Zetas*, the notorious narcotics trafficking gang down in Mexico had been committing such atrocities long before the world even knew who ISIS was. Furthermore, notorious armed gangs such as *Los Zetas* and ISIS have been around ever since civilization developed isolated societies.

Although you are far more likely to confront, say, a trash bin fire or even a tornado than a terrorist attack, the latter remains far more likely to catch your organization completely off guard and lead to tremendous casualties. That both ISIS and narco-traffickers remain active in all fifty states of the United

States merely serves to underscore the potential for mass destruction.

Your organization's procedures section must be as broad and as in-depth as practicality allows. For example, an isolated small town in the Midwest should not plan for an airplane to crash into it even though such things happen all over the planet. A responsible threat assessment, conducted by a knowledgeable member of your team, will determine whether any one crisis is possible (*anything* is), probable, or likely and you will develop response measures accordingly.

As with a well-coached professional sports team, your personnel will respond to different situations with choreographed precision – hopefully. An approaching tornado may require teachers leading terrified students into a storm shelter. A large fire may require those same teachers to corral the students into the *correct* path to safety based upon where, precisely, that fire exists. Certain ushers in s church may rush to the aid of a stricken parishioner (obviously those with some form of medical training or who know which members are doctors, paramedics, nurses, etc.) while his or her partners quickly call for an ambulance, if the need should be required.

For its role, members of a hospital security team – whom heretofore in history have been preoccupied with checking badges – may have to handle the arrival of an agitated patient. The question remains, however, is this angry patient someone who is simply tired of waiting within the emergency room too long? Or a violent patient who wants to target the nurse he or she presumes did them a great injustice? There *must* be an authenticated procedure in place that can deescalate the confrontation whatever the situation.

Speaking of proper procedures, has *your* plan been reviewed by your legal team? That aggressive patient may hold deep-seated psychological issues that could land your facility in court should your personnel mishandle the situation altogether. Even relatively minor grievances can lead to significant problems if the plaintiff locates a willing trial lawyer. And you thought that security meant confronting armed aggressors exclusively. It is hereby offered that such trial attorneys have done more damage to the healthcare system than all the belligerent patients on the planet have.

Effective procedures must be constantly scrutinized and reevaluated. Your team must address the following considerations during your *weekly* security briefings:

1. Has this particular action been undertaken by anyone else before, especially within our field?

2. Have we ever encountered a situation in the past where this particular procedure may have offered some value if available back then?

3. If not, what are the prospects that our organization – or one similar to ours – will encounter the particular threats addressed by this action?

4. Do we possess the personnel and resources necessary to undertake this procedure and ensure its probable efficiency?

5. What are the liabilities that threaten us even if we conduct ourselves professionally and mitigate damage from the aggressor or

situation?

6. What might have we *overlooked*?

Few opportunities exist to think about actionably during crises, so your security team must meet and share thoughts during regular meetings. In fact, if your community defense team were to meet on different days throughout the month for its weekly meetings, the chances exist that such breaking the 'status quo' will lead to innovation and creative suggestions. This is only natural, for "weekly meetings" tend to suggest bureaucracy and few personnel care to attend them.

In situations where significant threats appear, such as active shooter incidents, there remains the strong possibility that your 'front line' defense team will suffer casualties. This is just part of life; the worst things often happen even to those who are best able to deal with such occurrences. Whether or not your 'second tier' staff – or perhaps standby volunteers – can quickly adjust to the situation may mean the difference between life and death. Therefore, what procedures have you made to ensure that even the "worst" would not become the *last*?

During the September 11, 2001 attacks, most of the experienced first responders in New York City were killed during the collapse of the Twin Towers of the World Trade Center. This left firefighters and medical personnel severely handicapped for dealing with subsequent injuries. Today, that singular event changed the way that first responders react to calls for assistance. Your community, unfortunately, does not represent an entire profession. At best, you may only have a few people to place into your security defense team.

Therefore, your procedures section must go well beyond simply telling your team what to do in planned crises. Beforehand, it must instruct your members on *who*, within your overall organization, is best to fill in during any given time. This means that he or she not only needs to act as a recruiter, but as an impromptu instructor as well. While the reasoning behind redundancy is obvious, the purpose behind your members – rather than its leadership – undertaking this function may not be.

First, this brief exercise in personnel delegation keeps the thought of "others filling in" during crises alive. Second, it places those with the most experience free to ascertain *who* is best to fill in during such crises. Finally, and perhaps most importantly, it keeps the concept of security and defense evolving. Too many great plans fail because people grow tired of the project and its implementation rests with a solitary individual. For your community to survive crises, *everyone* must be involved even if he or she is not an active member of the security team.

Your procedures section must define who holds responsibility for specific functions, who *may* fill in during shortages, what equipment is allotted for certain activities, what level of training is required to turn your community into a defender instead of a casualty, and, perhaps most importantly of all, what their specific physical security measures entail.

PHYSICAL MEASURES

Heretofore, most of what has been discussed represents the intangible aspects of security and defense, elements designed primarily to foster a mindset of survival. Realistically, however, security represents a *physical* discipline, one involving both passive structural fabrications *and* active response measures. For your community's defense, you must shore both these physical barriers to aggression. This is not to say that both considerations must be equal, for your school, hospital, or church's architectural design may be out of your present influence. Rather, that you must achieve the most out of what you can work with.

If your church or school were, for instance, a registered national landmark, then, obviously, you could not tear down walls to build new security corridors or safe rooms. Accordingly, your function would shift towards more proactive, incident-specific responses given escalating threats. In regard, your team would train less on how to make your *structure* more secure, but rather its environment. On the other hand, if you were influential in the building of a new school or church, then your team could meet with the chief architect and request specific design features to allow a smaller response team.

Physical security, for our intents and purposes, represents anything that an aggressor may come into direct contact with during his or her crime – doors, windows, walls, vehicles, dogs, thorny bushes, armed guards, irate grandmothers with a broom, etc. These measures are intended to serve two distinct yet complimentary functions: one, to detour the aggressor from penetrating your common space; and, two, to channel him or her away from your vital areas should he or she manage to penetrate your common space. That the aggressor may be dealt a lethal blow during the commission of his or her crime actually serves both of these tasks.

Given this duality of purpose, physical security remains best a systems approach and, as such, must be integral to your tactical plan. It represents the playing field upon which your team exists and understands the duties and limitations of his or her position. As with a professional sports team, your physical environment mandates that members of your community security and defense program adhere to certain positions, behave within specific manners, and head towards a unified objective.

Consider, for instance, the following diagram:

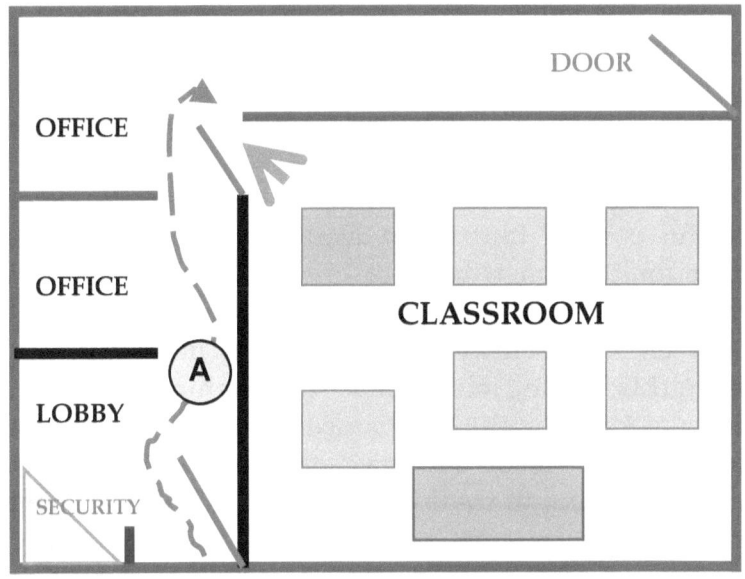

Figure 3. Simplified congested space.

In this illustration, we witness a very basic scenario in which an active shooter (A) enters a school in order to "kill as many people as he can". Under the usual circumstances, the students within the classroom would either barricade themselves into the classroom or try to escape and reach the outside. In this particular environment, however, you can see that this latter option remains dangerous, as the students would have to exit through the door and arrive in plain sight of the shooter if they were able to stand a chance of reaching the outer door at the right of the hallway.

There *may* be some beneficial turmoil if the shooter were to target employees residing in either or both of the offices, but this effectively sacrifices the employees or the students in order to save the other. Regardless of this scenario, casualties would arise unless personnel in the offices were possessing firearms and had sufficient time to react to the shooter (*someone* in either of the offices is probably going to be targeted before any employee with a firearm nearby would be able to respond).

Now, notice that we have placed a security desk in the corner, buttressed against the outside walls (presumably constructed of brick or some other solid material) with another partial, though steadfast wall between the security station and the main entrance. With this arrangement, any approaching shooter is likely to focus on the two immediate offices confronting their vision. He or she may even assume – perhaps correctly owing to traditional architecture – that one of the two offices *most visible* represents the facility's security office.

In this particular arrangement, the security team, already functioning within an alert manner, will see the shooter enter the building *before* he or she sees the facility's defensive posture. In this regard, security will have those precious seconds to respond before massive casualties erupt. You will also note, perhaps, that the left wall of the classroom and top lobby wall are sturdier than the others are. In this particular scenario, these walls are strengthened with dense sheathing so that, should the unfortunate occur, any shots taken by the security force (presumably with frangible ammunition) will not penetrate through the interior of the building and cause innocent casualties.

Most facilities – including hospitals and schools, although churches offer more flexibility – set their guard stations directly in front of the entrance doors, perhaps even sharing space with a receptionist. This represents a profound violation of practical security considerations, for *no one* should be able to observe a site's security arrangement *immediately*. This provides the aggressor with an advantage, as he or she may be able to predetermine where or how to conceal their weapon. With defensive personnel tucked securely in the corner, one of two things are likely to happen.

First, the aggressor will proceed as intended and security personnel will target them in turn.

Two, the aggressor will turn to focus on the security station, which will give trained employees in the offices a chance to target the aggressor.

Either of the above scenarios will permit students in the classroom to effect an escape while the aggressor tangles with security and/or staff. The point remains that a slight relocation of a security counter may produce extraordinary dividends in self-defense. At its foundation, this scheme adds *time* to the effort by having potential aggressors (and other suspicious persons) actually walk *past* a facility's first line of defense before being noticed. And time is *everything* in survival.

Whichever situation ultimately develops, the underlying similarity involves shots fired within a confined, vulnerable space (whether from the perpetrator or defenders). Because of this, intense planning much go into both architecture and incident protocol. Experts must be called in to ascertain damage done from ricocheting bullets, including to such ancillary systems such as electrical, sprinklers, plumbing, lighting, etc.

From the defender viewpoint, extensive considerations must be given towards *how* each individual reacts. In our scenario, if the security team shoots first, then they are firing into fixed, bullet-resistant (though not bulletproof) barriers. However, if the staff fires from the offices, then their field of firing rest drastically reduced, as they will have to consider the glass entry doors. This underscores the need for intense training and planning for *anyone* carrying firearms on premises.

In this last regard, *physical* measures include every aspect of your tactical doctrine where people, bullets, furniture, debris, etc. exist within your particular environment and such physical items are not stationary. This means that including within training measures, efforts to both move and *function* within a chaotic environment.

TRAINING

If you were to select one item out of your community's plan for survival, cherish it as if it were your last connection with the broader world, and devote every moment, every resource towards its implementation, then that particular subject would be *training*. This includes more than just the mere acquisition of knowledge; training, as a discipline, represents *drilled* instruction to ensure that the individual can repeat required actions even under the most demanding of situations.

These measures, which make military 'boot camp' so effective, condition the individual into responding to crises without thinking – itself a reaction that does little but force a person into hesitance. Actions must become secondary, *subconscious* functions where the objective is usually achieved before the individual even realizes that the activity has commenced.

When a person stumbles along the sidewalk, the action certainly catches him or her by surprise, yet they automatically recover (though, perhaps, slightly embarrassed) and quickly resume their normal stride. This individual does not stop and rationalize *why* they tripped, nor must they tell their legs to resume walking. None of this matters because, after years' worth of walking, the individual's subconscious mind *instinctively knows how to react whenever their feet are tangled.*

Such a subconscious adjustment for survival should be instilled within everyone within your community, especially those who hold responsibility for others' lives. In such life and death cases, delay *will* result in someone's death, even if you make it out intact.

Listen whenever a television news channel covers a recent shooting, regardless of where the incident occurred. Whether the episode covered a school shooting, gang-related 'drive by' murder, or, perhaps, a neighbor committing suicide; the witnesses interviewed by the media will declare the same thing. That the incident sounded as if a car backfiring, the handle of a broom breaking, or someone tipping over a trashcan – *anything* but the sound of a firearm discharged.

The reason for this omnipresent confusion rests upon the average person's unfamiliarity with firearms, despite their appearance on television shows and in motion pictures. The vast *majority* of the human population has never heard a gun fired, and therefore their minds have to fill in the blanks with sounds and noises that it understands. This is similar to sleeping within a new house where an individual never gets a decent night's rest because he or she is always alert to those strange noises that the mind desperately tries to squash as "the hot water heater" or "the water pump" or, simply, "settling". Back home, he or she sleeps soundly because their subconscious categorizes such sounds as *routine* – not worth waking the conscious mind about.

In your community – whether school, church, or hospital – such confusion, no matter how brief, will lead to disaster. Even if your personnel have never fired a gun in his or her life, they should become intimately aware with the sound various types of firearms make. Simply listening to movies on television will not work. He or she must attend a firing range, preferably one indoors (or as similar to their community environment as possible).

The recognition that results from such familiarization programs will initiate a 'spark' of action rather than reaction. In the time that it takes for the average individual to say, "Oh, *that* must be an automobile backfiring!" several individuals could be seriously harmed instead. You may not be sufficiently fast to save them, but you *must* be sufficiently quick-witted enough to save others. The key to "rendering the aggressor unable to inflict harm" is to ensure that his or her criminal progression ceases upon contact with you. As with a tackler in football, perhaps the only action that *you* can expect is to prevent forward progress until aid arrives.

This requires knowledge absorbed several ways:

- *Mētis.* This represents intuitive or experiential knowledge acquired from conducting the activity itself and primarily used to adjust to continuously changing environments such as that experienced by diplomats and athletes.[6]

- *Techne.* Obscure, technical knowledge one can learn without firsthand experience through segmented rules and procedures such as mathematical formulae or cooking recipes.[7]

- *Epiphany.* As the name suggests, an individual will, on occasion, suddenly develop insight or solution towards a particular problem. Usually, this involves both *Métis* and *Techne* to a combination of degrees as very few individuals can come to a realization on any subject without previous calculation or exposure.

Your tactical plan must allow your team to acquire training from all these avenues through the proper *inspiration* to learn – something that even most colleges and universities today fail to provide.

Mētis learning results when members of your staff freely exchange ideas and experiences towards with which others may learn or experiment. This may

---

[6] Michael Kenney, *From Pablo to Osama: Trafficking and Terrorist Networks, Government Bureaucracies, and Competitive Adaptation* (University Park, PA: The Pennsylvania State University Press, 2007), 4.
[7] Ibid., 82.

further lead to competitive adaptation if one person's "war stories" motivate another to recall an even better kernel of knowledge about a particular subject. Videos and DVDs also allow members of your security team to acquire experiential knowledge from experts outside your staff. For example, the American Gunsmithing Institute (AGI) offers numerous armorer's courses providing quality instruction on how various firearms function. The student or viewer should possess one of the firearms in order to maximize the value of the course, but simply watching these low-cost DVDs provides a great deal of knowledge about the workings of the most popular firearms available (which, if anything, will reduce ignorance and hysteria regarding guns).

The learning opportunities from *Techne* are less complicated, merely requiring a set of instructions and the prospects of a motivated individual to understand them adequately. For example, you may possess specific instructions for fires, tornadoes, and snowstorms in addition to procedures in place for active shooters, terrorism, and civil disobedience. That these actions probably resulted from vast experiential knowledge matters very little; they can be taught through written instruction.

Your community's tactical plan must never exclude sources of knowledge or the mechanisms through which such information is shared (something that a great many municipal and federal agencies violate). Training remains at the heart of your plan and learning rests as the foundation of this requirement. To dismiss knowledge acquired from one source or method above another places *everyone* into harm's way. Instead of restricting information, you must endorse every aspect of it to ensure that *training* is not irreparably harmed.

SUPPLEMENTAL DATA

The final section of your tactical plan represents everything "else" that may not fit neatly into any of the foregoing divisions. This "catch all" section serves as the primary reason that your plan is kept within a three-ring binder, to ensure that additions and subtractions can be made during the lifetime of your community's efforts to secure it against threats.

A supplemental data sheet may, for instance, involve a change in security uniforms from the ineffective (but appealing) blazers to more noticeable (but intimidating) military fatigues. In general, the following items should be reserved for this final section of your tactical plan:

- Equipment or uniform changes.

- Maps, diagrams, or charts.

- Changes to community property that may affect future tactical plans (e.g., the construction of a new swimming pool that may create a new procedures sheet).

- Marketing brochures and pamphlets from potential suppliers, contractors, etc.

- Pending vacations or "off time" of critical personnel (of a duration that will not affect the personnel disposition section).

- Research data on emerging threats and/or innovative procedures from other communities.

- Recommended reading lists (in order to not affect the training section).

- Important telephone numbers, contact names, and other transitory communications.

- Copies of any document subsequently modified or deleted from the record (for reference and liability purposes and generally removed after three years).

As designed, the supplemental data section provides your tactical plan with the potential for alteration without the need to have such information continuously approved by management as within the previous sections. That said, this section should not become a 'trash bin' of scrap unimportant to the plan itself.

6. PERSONNEL

WITH a proper tactical action plan in place, the next step for your community remains filling the various roles required for security and defense of your particular establishment. You may have already recruited many of the key people needed to write the procedures and outline the responsibilities for your group, but overall you have not had much time to delve deeper into involving *everyone* that comes into contact with your surroundings. You may not even have considered the participation of employees, students, patients, deacons, or anyone else that may periodically occupy your school, hospital, or church.

Nevertheless, *people* make or break your defense. They represent the "first observers" whose function remains far more important than the first responders who only arrive *after* a critical incident has taken place. With the national average for police response within the United States to range from fifteen to *forty-five* minutes, any individual that can aid you should be considered as a fundamental element of your community's defense, even if he or she is not aware of their participation. We shall discuss this clandestine "recruitment" in a moment. For now, we must focus on those individuals that retain some measure of responsibility for others' safety.

To begin with, we can isolate the "perfect" type of individual that any community security or defense effort should retain. These individuals bear the following characteristics:

1. Above average intelligence combined with strong commonsense;

2. Proficient in martial subjects and skills (global politics, martial arts, hunting, outdoor activities, etc.);

3. Possessing good judgment and an even temperament;

4. Patient, curious, innovative, creative, confident, and somewhat analytical;

5. Loyal, reliable, strong team player, and courageous;

6. Physically and mentally fit, tough, alert, and determined;

7. Possessing excellent coordination and rational movement;

8. Of overall excellent health and free from such vices as drinking, smoking, chewing, etc.

That few individuals, perhaps, carry all of these characteristics, these should nevertheless represent the pantheon by which all personnel are judged, for it is always best to strive for perfection and fall a bit short than, as the saying goes, settle for inferiority and ultimately reach that goal.

In order to do this, particularly within a field as dynamic and critical as security and defense, we must first understand the probabilities for human action. That is, *how* he or she is likely to function with perceivable threats in mind. The following illustration allows for such judgment, bearing in mind that if rules retain exception, then certainly people bear rule-shattering exceptions as well.

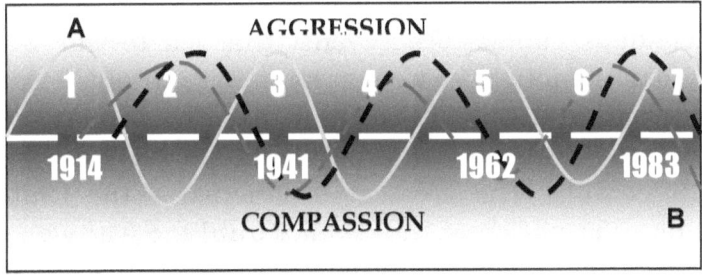

Figure 4. Pattern of conflict and peace in relationship to human reaction.

In Figure 4, we observe how two groups of individuals react in relationship to conflict along a progression of history (white dotted line) from an initial point of maximum conflict (A) towards a declining equilibrium when warfare and society begin to collapse (B). Numbers indicate opposing shifts in war and dates exemplify notable conflicts. The gray solid line represents the cyclic nature of conflict whereas the dark gray dashed line (interventionists) and black dashed line (isolationists) represents the two representative personality types of our discussion.

You will note two quick observations. First, the interventionists remain quicker to engage within war when compared with the isolationists, despite both group's lagging behind the emergence of aggression.

Second, as time progresses, both groups increase their perception of pending conflicts, even though neither side swings into full synchronization. To better understand this, let us turn to the historical dates identified within the graph.

1914. The start of World War I represents a critical year, which is why we have chosen it for our exemplary date. From the perspective of the future, we can recall the various triggers that led to this horrendous conflict. The events that led to war were singular enough to, perhaps, restraint most participants. Even those that eagerly sought war incorrectly assumed that it would be an extremely short conflict. The greatest isolationist – the United States – did not enter the conflict until the war was on its final legs (indeed entering the conflict just in time for its final year).

1941. The year 1941 does not particularly represent the worst year of the Second World War, but it does represent the year Japan decided to inaugurate the planet's first *true* global war. Here, we noticed that both isolationists and interventionists were unprepared for war despite both as having been eager during the interwar period. Two factors support this analysis. First, the Western militaries, such as the United States, were active in Latin America or in Northern Africa during the years following the First World War. Second, even the U.S. Navy was actually conducting "bombing raids" upon Hawaii as early as 1932 in preparation for conflict. Yet, by 1941, France, Britain, and the United States, all economic powerhouses, had *lost* armies during the opening years of the conflict. The buildups prior to 1941 – such as the Maginot Line in France – did little to prevent actual conflict.

1962. The Cuban Missile Crisis of 1962 placed the world on the verge of instant nuclear war for the very first time in history. Nevertheless, the existence of both WWII and the Korean Conflict did little to promote or sustain preparedness for war. Isolationists, through heroic efforts during the Korean War and fascination with the forthcoming struggle in Vietnam, retained concern for the heightening Cold War with the Soviet Union. For their role, the interventionists of previous world wars and Korean Conflict (with, especially, the Democratic Party of the U.S. in complete control) seemingly grew dissatisfied with conflict by the middle of the 1960s and, more or less, found equilibrium based mostly upon *internal intervention* under the guise of civil rights protests.

1983. For the first time since the Cuban Missile Crisis, the world sat on the verge of all-out nuclear war, an experience predicated upon the Soviet's perception that American president Ronald Reagan remained a stark raving mad "Cowboy" set on launching war himself. Combined with the later shooting down of Korean Airlines Flight 007 during the year, both interventionists and isolationists remained prepared for any conflict, riding upon the extremely popular election of President Reagan. It was the collapse of the Soviet Union by 1991 that ushered in an era where the world began to settle down into a less-intensive realization of casual war. Despite recent conflicts in places such as Iraq, Afghanistan, etc. we have been riding this period of equilibrium ever since.

Your role in selecting people for your community's defense program must consider how "deeply polarized" people will sour your chances for lasting security. That is, you want neither people like in 1914 that remain slow to accept conflict nor people like those living in 1941 that, while prepared, were nowhere near ready to fight when aggressors show up delivery sneak attacks. People naturally react *too early* or in a manner at opposites with what needs doing.

This, in effect, goes back to Gideon's weaning of the thousands into a mere 300 souls willing to remain alert when conflict beckons. In your case, you do not even need that 300. With intelligence, street smarts, a gift for understanding the news (and not the news media), and, finally, fit enough to cover distances within your facility without collapsing from fatigue, any individual can be trained and motivated to protect.

You do, however, have to keep the above graph in perspective; most people will either retreat from threats or act *only* when everyone else does. Telling the future is impossible. That said, what you need are people who can perceive the future. This is *not* impossible because Old West gunfighters, gamblers, and even decent stockbrokers do it. For instance, if you see cities turn to rioting on the television because of police backing down, then you can ascertain similar actions for your local community. *Eventually.*

Your town may erupt into flames tomorrow. Or, perhaps, three years from today. Where the concern rests is that *eventually*, everything happens to your local environment. From a broader context, we can observe the past three decades – indeed, going back even to the 1979 Islamic Revolution in Iran. Many people are quite familiar with the events in Teheran, but few are familiar with the simultaneous attack on

U.S. facilities in Pakistan. At any rate, the revolution inspired by the Ayatollah Khomeini led to desires for revolution in other parts of the Middle East.

This resentment towards invaders – especially "infidels" – following the Soviet invasion of Afghanistan exacerbated the situation, leading to the rise of fanatics that took Khomeini's "message" and used it to destroy *anything* that did not support that particular vision. This, in turn, resulted in the mass exodus of millions of Muslims from the Middle East. If researchers such as Dr. Stanley Milgram *proved* that sixty-five percent (65%) of people *could* be induced into killing innocent human beings with little prompting from an authoritative figure, then we have to assume that the majority of these fleeing Muslims, as with all other groups, retain the *potential* for killing.

Unfortunately, this mass exodus of Muslims from the chaotic Middle East means that the migration is moving too fast either for, say, European immigration authorities to handle or for the arriving individuals to assimilate effectively. This causes a sharp "clash of civilizations" that infuriates most and instigates a few. These "few" turn towards that authoritative figure in the guise of Muhammad and Allah and begin to kill because his or her actions transcend earthly restrictions.

Now, with the situation in Europe bulging with fleeing Muslims, the immigrants begin to seek asylum elsewhere, such as within the United States and Canada. It will not be long before the entire process begins anew here and the authorities will not be able to handle anything that threatens the status quo that law enforcement doctrine is designed to manage. Americans, for their role, cannot dismiss this activity as "foreign" either, for the same crisis exists on the southern border of the U.S. Millions of illegal immigrants have crossed that border, most seeking a better life away from the chaos in Mexico. However, a great many thousands – by virtue of his or her involvement within the narcotics trade, weapons trafficking, terrorism, etc. – come into the United States seeking profit and power *illicitly.*

This crisis led one researcher to suggest that the entire American Southwest may descend into something akin to a "Waziristan, U.S.A."[8] One only has to consider the roughly 400,000 actionable police officers within the United States to feel that the trend tilts heavily in the criminals' favor. This is *precisely* the reason that your community needs individuals that can read the proverbial handwriting on the wall and adjust accordingly.

He or she must be able to peer through the hyperbole offered by politicians on the television and the conspiratorial rants found on social media and ascertain the best prospects for your weathering of what is coming down the pike. This requires a fundamental understanding of history, human interaction, and a mind tactical enough to develop strategies to deal with various scenarios affecting *your* community. Those pundits on the news or amateur sociologists on the Web do *not* have your community's best interests at heart.

Security represents one of the few fields where it is quite legitimate to remain xenophobic to the point where isolation and suspicion of others is the preferred way of doing things. During concealed-carry classes,

---

[8] Paul Rexton Kan, *Mexico's "Narco-Refugees": The Looming Challenge for U.S. National Security* (Carlisle, PA: Strategic Studies Institute, October 2011), 25.

for example, students learn to challenge anyone inquiring of the time because *any* pedestrian on the street may use such ploys to enter your personal safety zone.

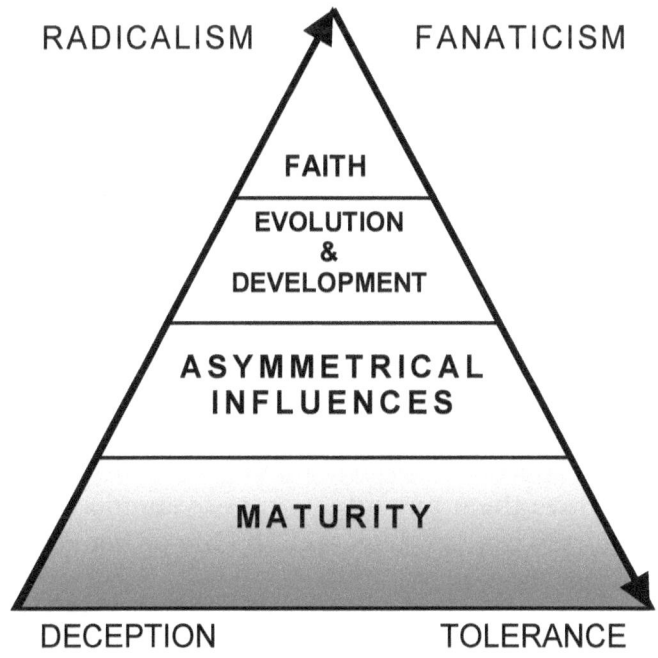

Figure 5. Pyramid of Radicalism. Adapted from R.J. Godlewski, "Human Intelligence: Perceiving an Enemy's Thoughts" *American Intelligence Journal 27, No. 1* (2009): 35.

As depicted within Figure 5, we can observe how individuals become fanatical in his or her beliefs. The driving force behind radicalization represents the individual's faith in their ideology, whether that is religious, political, or sociological. As the individual builds upon his or her maturity, they learn to acquire influence from a range of sources, evolving to a more personal appreciation of that faith. However, as we observe, the more fanatical an individual becomes, the less tolerant he or she remains; the more radical they are, the less capable they are of deceiving others.

These twin facets of radicalism work to aid those defending communities, for it remains exceedingly difficult for aggressors to *permanently* shield his or her intent from the observant. *Something* about their behavior, communication with others, and skin tone (yes, skin fluctuates with mood) will betray his or her mindset. This is why some cats will rear up and scowl at strangers they do not particularly trust.

To instill this ability within your team, select individuals that are comfortable with mingling amongst crowds and have them practice trying to ascertain the thoughts of shoppers and other pedestrians. Clothing stores are good environments for this, as it remains relatively easy to perceive thoughts such as an individual preferring one style or color over another. Have them pay attention to bystanders too, to see if spouses remain detectable by his or her reaction towards the shopper.

This falls into the concept of intelligence – gathering as much information as useful about your adversaries. The counterpart to this involves *counterintelligence* – ensuring that your threats do not obtain any information about *your* community. Accordingly, your security and defense team must focus, perhaps, more on keeping information out of the hands of aggressors than learning about potential threats. This is definitely not easy for individuals, yet it is imperative since you are more likely to encounter "intelligence leaks" than terrorists trying to target your facility for destruction.

7. INTELLIGENCE & COUNTERINTELLIGENCE

HAVING selected your leadership and support personnel, your community must continue to hone its intelligence and counterintelligence abilities, something that remains quite suited for non-governmental organizations planted within the population. Here is where *you* offer prospects for success (and survival) beyond the limitations of both federal and municipal police agencies.

The U.S. correctional system offers a case study to scrutinize. This population of exclusively criminal individuals holds a vast reservoir of data regarding illicit organizations and practices and, yet, the law enforcement community remains hesitant to tap into this pool of intelligence.[9] Of what major revelations await the security-conscious individual who attempts to pick the minds of such career felons? Naturally, members of a school, hospital, or church cannot expect to visit prisons just to learn about criminal activity. That is *not* the issue.

School staff must be aware of what rests within

---

[9] See "Case Study: Creating Intelligence Systems in Corrections", Stan Stojkovic, David Kalinich, and John Klofas, *Criminal Justice Organizations: Administration and Management, Fifth Edition* (Belmont, CA: Wadsworth, 2012), 124-125.

his or her community. Hospital employees must be aware of how terrorists are learning about emergency medical response procedures and radio communications. Church ushers need to suspect that the relative "openness" of religious facilities is *precisely* the reason they are targeted by anyone with a grievance or a cause to promote.

Simply *knowing* is not productive; an individual must hold to learning – a continual process to evaluate what was learned yesterday while retaining the foresight to anticipate what tomorrow offers us. In other words, your knowledge is only as good as your education and your education is only as good as your imagination. You must always *learn* rather than rely upon remaining "taught" exclusively.

This tugs somewhat at the popularized dictum that "knowledge is power". While essentially true, the ability to generate knowledge exceeds the value of storing information. It is also a two-way street. For example, it *may* do you no harm if a particular adversary holds *some* knowledge about you, your family, or your neighborhood. However, if he or she were able to increase that knowledge – that is, through the *generation* of intelligence – then that will eventually irreparably harm your safety.

This implies that intelligence *and* counterintelligence go hand in hand and that assessment remains valid. Unfortunately, a great many people, even within the national Intelligence Community (e.g, CIA, FBI, NSA, etc.), split the two disciplines into separate fields managed by disparate groups. Fortunately for you, your community is undoubtedly too small and under-resourced to pay people to simply walk the halls bored or partake of "Diversity Quilt" human tolerance programs. *Anyone within your employ must be security-conscious at all levels.*

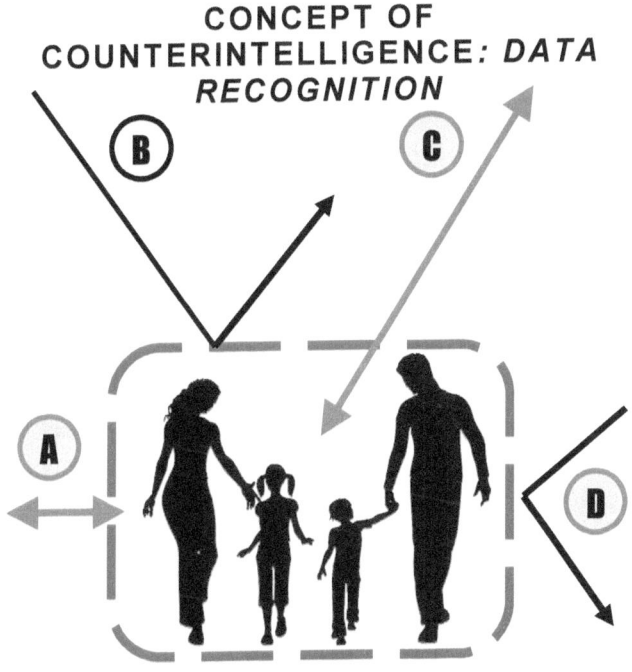

Figure 6. How counterintelligence can aid families.
Silhouette image: © Kirsty Pargeter - Fotolia.com

Let us look at several scenarios involving Figure 6 and observe how an ordinary family may employ counterintelligence functions to safeguard their information and their lives from predators. In our scenarios, the dotted box around the family represents their security consciousness – or counterintelligence awareness – that sifts out information concerning the husband and wife as well as regarding their young children. The arrowed lines represent information flow.

If A, for instance, represented a legitimate credit card purchase made by the wife, then the two-way flow of information has been authenticated and permitted to reach the consumer prior to heading back out to the retailer. The same would be the case if C represented the girl's birthday card received from a grandmother, in which case her appreciative reply would be acceptable communication.

On the suspicious side, suppose that B represented a "frequent shopper" card from the local grocer. At face value, this represents a relatively common – and presumably "safe" – transaction. Yet, *once that information leaves your control*, the supermarket company can share that information with just about *anyone* (who bothers to read all that fine print that allows the manufacturer to disclose that information?). Ever visit Amazon.com and, perhaps, check emails through Yahoo only to discover suggestions based upon the very books that you just ordered? That advertisement from Amazon.com resulted from information shared with Yahoo (or whichever service you employ).

If D represented a survey from a national research company or political organization, the information could be used in much the same way. Except this time, there would be no fine print to read. In fact, you *cannot* know if such a research organization or political body were the actual telephone caller. Most advertising agencies, skip tracers, collection firms, and dozens of other businesses understand how to fake Caller ID data to suggest that your telephone call comes, not from them, but, perhaps, your closet friend and confidant. For this reason, both the grocery store discount card and marketing survey telephone call represent too much trouble to accommodate.

Any information – or data – that you do not

recognize (i.e., control) should be considered a potential threat and dismissed without response. At a minimum, this will reduce the number of automated telephone calls that you are likely to receive since once you answer any computer's call; it will automatically share your number with thousands of other marketing robots as a valid residence or office number with which to pitch their client's wares.

For your community, however, you must endure a greater effort to secure compromising information about your particular environment. Some of the site-specific counterintelligence issues that you need to address include:

For Schools. Schools, as members of the public environment, undertake a great deal of marketing to promote their sports teams, fund-raising efforts, and musical productions. Unfortunately, this provides criminals, disgruntled ex-spouses, and other malcontents with a range of information he or she may use to harm individuals or, at a minimum, sabotage that institution's reputation. Care must be taken whenever such promotional material is released.

For example, a great many (if not vast majority of) secondary schools provide parents of honors students with those ubiquitous bumper stickers attesting to their children's academic prowess. These advertisements simply provide perpetrators with easy access to which residences possess young schoolchildren, by which they can survey a car in any parking lot or home and plan, perhaps, for abduction simply because the school provided them with a direct *connection* between home and place of education. This grants the criminal an opportunity to plan for a more advantageous abduction by allowing them to seek out further vulnerabilities.

A second concern involves school fundraising activities such as door-to-door candy sales or even corner carwashes. In either case, the event exposes both the school and the student to observation by suspicious characters. For instance, selling candy bars door to door announces which child within the neighborhood belongs to which particular school (and undoubtedly parent, if he or she "escorts" the student). This exposes, amongst other details, the relative age of the child, what his or her bus schedule is likely to be, and which extracurricular activities the would-be abductor should focus upon.

Fundraising car washes, for their role, offer a criminal an opportunity to spy on his or her prey from a vantage point. Usually, such carwashes represent a flurry of activity within a retail location that naturally draws numerous cars and shoppers. Few remain observant enough to consider if another individual is paying far too much attention on the festivities usually associated with such an event. Worse still, the mere nature of the activity persuades young girls to "dress down", thereby exposing them to even greater scrutiny by an aggressive perpetrator that may even be wielding a camera.

Because of their position within society and an almost guaranteed lack of suitable funding, schools represent a "positive" flow of information – meaning that they speak volumes about their students while doing relatively little to squash that data exchange. With the advent of notebook computers and cell phones in the classroom, the asymmetrical advantage tossed towards technology-savvy criminals merely increases the threat significantly.

For Hospitals. Once the hallmark of religious and educational institutions, state and county hospitals turned the healing and service of the sick into a broad bureaucratic healthcare industry replete with specialty clinics, extraordinarily complex insurance plans, and a vast transportation system designed to extract patients from various predicaments and move them to where assistance is best. The arrival of modern information and communications technology simply means that this vast world of medicine is as interconnected as possible.

Sadly, all this marvelous innovation has simply exposed patients to greater dangers than, perhaps, his or her original condition. Once drab buildings that everyone knew about but few cared to admit, hospitals have become business powerhouses that routinely advertise on television to attract patients and increase their corporate bottom line. With every patient admitted or serviced, even a small healthcare clinic's data reservoir increases by several billion bits. Patient records, now stored electronically, carry the virtual life history of that man or woman, including their prescription records, accident history, allergies, and a host of other personal information that could be used for illicit purposes (such as assassinating a prominent individual simply by hacking into the hospital's computer database to alter his or her medication).

Some notable efforts to misuse information from the healthcare and emergency medical professions by individuals with illicit intent include:

Emergency Service Operations:

- April, 2007, a Middle Eastern subject in Dekalb County, Indiana enrolled within an Emergency

Medical Technician (EMT) class appeared more interested within hospital operations involving "secondary devices" and "terrorism" than EMT procedures; [10]

- December 2007, two males of Middle Eastern descent enrolled within Indianapolis EMT courses exhibited suspicious activity, preferring to understand the concepts of hospital emergency communications and response measures than those subjects that were required for their actual certification;[11]

- February 2008, subjects claiming to be "foreign doctors" with unlimited funds inquired on the availability of private fast-track ambulance driving licensure in Las Vegas, Nevada;

Hospital Operations

- October 2007, hospital security staff in Maywood, Illinois filed report regarding suspicious males driving yellow rental truck and discussing their location as "ground zero";[12]

- January 2008, two Middle Eastern men videotaped the interior of Indianapolis hospital, departing the presence when they could not satisfactorily identify themselves to security personnel;[13]

---

[10] Indiana Department of Homeland Security/Indiana Intelligence Fusion Center, *Suspicious Activity Involving Emergency Services and Hospitals*, June 2008.
[11] Ibid.
[12] Ibid.
[13] Ibid.

- The November 2008 terrorist siege in Mumbai, India, which killed 166 people and left hundreds injured, specifically targeted Cama & Albless Hospital;[14]

- In 2007, members of the Arellano-Felix drug cartel stormed a Tijuana, Hospital targeting a rival cartel member. Two police officers were killed in the attack;[15]

These trends are expected to increase.

In Israel, for instance, ambulances are routinely inspected prior to gaining access to hospitals and clinics. We shall discuss these precautions in the appropriate chapter of this book. For now, however, the above suffices to suggest the extraordinary (if somewhat obvious) methods by which criminals and terrorists seek to gain intelligence about hospitals and healthcare operations.

Nevertheless, any hospital or healthcare setting, even within the relatively "peaceful" United States, has lost its shield of sanctity. Aggressors naturally seek the vulnerable and there remain fewer vulnerable people than those working or staying within a hospital. For this reason, criminals will spend a great deal of time ascertaining the security presence, schedules, deliveries, and pedestrian traffic associated with these facilities, unless you can deny them access to such information.

---

[14] D.J. Phalen, "Violence Against Hospitals Around the Globe and Healthcare Force Protection: Protecting Those Who Save Lives" in *Journal of Counterterrorism & Homeland Security International* 17, No. 2 (2001), p. 25.
[15] Ibid.

For Religious Facilities. If hospitals have lost their semblance of virtue, then religious institutions – particularly churches and synagogues – remain within the same consideration by criminals and terrorists, if not more so. Churches, as exemplified by the June 17, 2015 massacre at the Emanuel African Methodist Episcopal Church in Charleston, South Carolina, remain "open" facilities that, by their very nature, do not turn away even suspicious personnel.

For counterintelligence purposes, religious facilities represent an absolute nightmare. That said, certain sects such as the Church of Jesus Christ of Latter-day Saints (or Mormons) and the Church of Scientology do possess *extraordinary* counterintelligence functions to keep their activities away from scrutiny. However, such actions, with all due common sense, border more upon the cultish than faithful aspects of what Westerners normally declare to represent a religious body.

For most congregations, religious facilities remain open – even promoted as such – so that any individual can enter to be "saved" or enlightened as the case may be. The relative freedom of movement and communication sends shivers up the spine of security professionals. How, for instance, can one protect the congregation of a church when bulletins announce the timing of services, signs identify the faith, and doors are held open for hundreds, if not thousands, of parishioners to come and go as he or she sees fit.

One Oklahoma church, as an example, wisely chose not to broadcast the code for its new security locks (a measure taken after a recent burglary) and instead repeated the number for those in attendance during Mass. That said, who was to say that a criminal, surveying the church for a possible strike, was not in attendance? A gunman that had already been sitting within the church before he erupted into his rage undertook the Charleston shooting. Could it be unimaginable that another, perhaps less violent criminal, may have been sitting during Mass in Oklahoma (that had *already* experienced a burglary) when that parish priest announced the new security code for the church's front doors?

Part of the reason for the relative lack of security surrounding religious facilities represents the popular belief that "God protects" those in churches, synagogues, mosques, etc. Little is mentioned, apparently, that maybe God intends to use security professionals (or, at a minimum, security-conscious amateurs) to protect those churches. Instead, most religious personnel simply assume that *others* care enough about them to avoid causing harm. A great many martyrs litter history simply because they were killed *precisely* for being members of a religious faith.

How, then, does a church or other religious facility begin to employ counterintelligence within its ranks? First, it remains unlikely that religious institutions are going to refrain from advertising their schedules or public meetings. Second, there is very little reason to suspect that they will secure their doors with metal detectors or restrict attendance to card-carrying members of their faith. With these assumptions in mind, we can ascertain several policies that *may* alleviate the exposure of that particular religious function.

One way, is to reduce the description of planned activities. For example, terms such as "Senior Pot Luck Dinner" and "Teen's Night Out!" expose attendees to criminals that seek out specific targets. Perhaps such innocuous terms as "Silver Picnic" or "Mild Wild!", respectively, would diminish such information giveaways. The trick, particularly within the latter example, is to obtain suggestions from potential arrivals as to what he and she prefers to call their gathering. As social creatures, people just love to create new terms for old things and to offer what no one else does even if it actually represents the "same old thing." Such may offer to shield highly vulnerable events with little or no additional expenditures.

We have only *briefly* touched upon the concept of counterintelligence as it applies to schools, hospitals, and religious institutions. This was done in order to place protecting information at the foundation of a community's desire to protect itself. We shall now return towards discussing *intelligence* as protecting one is only half of the battle; defenders must also *weaken* his or her adversary. This means that you must learn as much about potential threats as possible – and they *will* be employing counterintelligence programs too.

Your best tactic is to begin broadly with international threats and then carefully bring your intelligence collection homeward while increasing in depth and specificity. In doing this, you shall group your knowledge into three distinct parameters, according to the "actionability" afforded by the threat: strategic intelligence, tactical intelligence, and crisis intelligence. The strategic intelligence sphere (all threat potentials are 360°) represents all those groups and individuals that answer the rhetorical question of "What threats have I *overlooked* before?" For the tactical sphere, this question turns to "What *could* be threatening my particular facility or community?"

Finally, at the crisis level, we ask of ourselves "How can anyone within my community or environment be in *immediate* danger?"

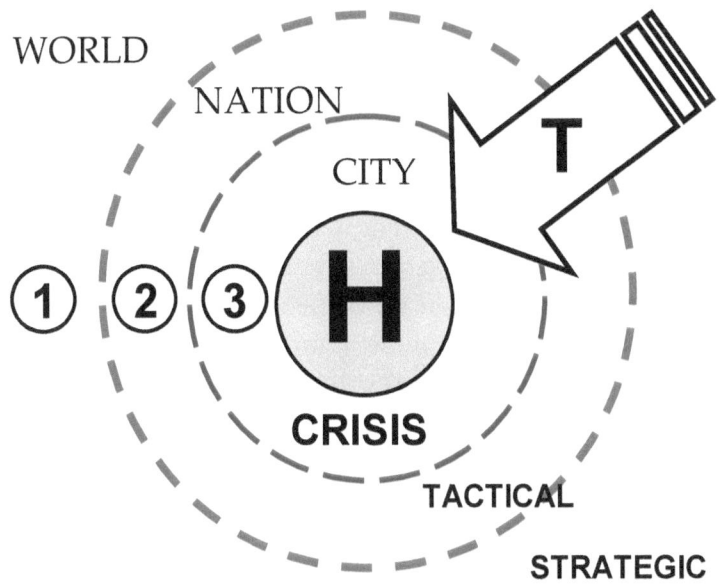

Figure 7. Intelligence perimeters for a hospital.

In Figure 7, we can observe how threats require elevated responses as they approach a particular community, in this case representing a hospital. At the outermost sphere, we remain concerned about strategic issues that affect the entire planet. We want to know about groups attacking other institutions and the existence of individuals that may lead to copycat or inspired attacks. This level of intelligence gathering, for your community, consists of, perhaps, little more than listening to the television news and visiting the Internet. For universities and colleges, this may mean interviewing foreign exchange students and applicants.

Focusing upon the strategic perspective means that your community remains hovering within Condition 1 – a state of mind shared with the rest of the planet. That is, you know that "things" happen in the broader world, but they remain just stories, similar to knowing that NASA has just sent a probe past Pluto. Interesting to know, but not important to your situation. Yet, you retain the knowledge because it might make you sound more intelligent among your peers.

When threats appear within your nation, they immediately take on more urgency, resulting in the acquisition of tactical intelligence. At this point, your focus shifts to Condition 2 – things are *happening* to individuals and institutions that share an affinity with you. For instance, say, that you live in economically troubled Detroit. You watched the events happen in Baltimore during April 2015 because they occurred in a city of like-minded people within your own country. You also know that what happens within any city quickly erupts into other cities as the events are often triggered by progenitors that seek out virgin municipalities to burn.

On occasion, such as in Seattle of 1999 during the Black Bloc anarchist protests against the World Trade Organization (WTO) meeting, or of the aforementioned Baltimore of 2015, events simply erupt within *your* town, irrespective of whether they migrated in from overseas or not. Here you emerge into Condition 3, a full-blown local crisis, and any intelligence gathering tends to be of the post-event, forensic variety slated to aid *future* response more than solving the current predicament.

Yet, Condition 3 does not automatically mean that *your* community is targeted. Again, this simply means that you must isolate immediate threats to your facility from those targeting neighborhood schools, churches, and hospitals. As with active shooter incidents involving nearby locations, your particular facility may be locked down in order to keep your people from haphazardly walking into a killing spree. This immediate threat is not an *actionable one*, meaning that your priority retreats towards protection rather than defense.

Unfortunately, as you and your staff scurry about locking doors, windows, and taking census of your students, staff, or congregation, you do *not* have time to write down specifics such as time of day, number of cars passing your driveway, or, perhaps, the hair color of pedestrians unaffected by the relative chaos within the city. At this point, intelligence-collection becomes a burden – even if you possess enough people for one to devote his or her entire day to such a topic.

For this reason in particular, you must take advantage of those "peaceful" times that exist in Conditions 1 and 2. You must function as if Condition 3 *will* happen at some point and your job is to meet it head-on when it does occur – even if that may be several years into the future.

During non-critical periods, your community's intelligence team must intimately understand the experiences of comparable institutions around the world. If a terrorist bombing happens in Madrid, then you must ask yourself how it would influence you where you and your friends live. If, say, Tokyo experienced another poison gas attack, you should immediately retrieve your tactical plan and record as many details of that event as you could enter into the Supplemental Data section and *quickly analyze that*

*information to see if procedural changes must be made
for your facility.*

Your involvement in intelligence is not to spy
nor even to stop spies; your function is to accumulate
as much actionable information as possible about the
threats that may target you in the future. With this
knowledge, you must classify it into varying degrees of
probability and then adjust your tactical plan
accordingly. Nevertheless, your fundamental intent
remains to place that information *into use.* In other
words, what would you *do* if the day occurs when the
international media will soon be knocking on your
institution's doors?

8. WAR!

YOU are seated comfortably at your desk when your guidance counselor rushes into the office screaming, "There is a mad gunman running down the hallway shooting *everyone* that he sees." What does this mean? You are kindly directing parishioners into the pews when you notice a strange woman, too heavily clothed for the season, stand up in the middle of the church and cry out "*Allah Akbar!*" What does this mean? You are walking towards the parking lot after a long shift in the ER and out of the peripheral of your vision; you observe a "strange" ambulance racing towards the hospital structure and *not* the emergency entrance. What does it mean?

All three cases mentioned above mean the exact same thing: *war* has come to your community. It may last as comparatively quick as the homicide bomber in the church or a bit longer as with the case of the speeding ambulance, but from that moment onwards life for you, your co-workers, your students, or your patients rests forever altered by combat enacted against your otherwise peaceful community.

Within those *very few* seconds, your entire life reduces to only one of those four damning actions: fight, flight, posture, or submit. In either of the above cases, *posturing* represents a moot point. Even

Superman would fail if he arrived *after* the fact. And in the real world, our "supermen" remain none other than the police and firefighters – but they, too, arrive after an attack. Submission is hard to bear for no other reason than the victims did *not* have a chance to choose his or her actions. To flee merely compounds this extreme guilt that you will experience as soon as you turn on the television news and see the hordes of stretchers carted off into ambulances or the fields of covered figures, lying permanently silenced beneath blankets.

Despite popular opinion, war is not merely something that debating politicians declare whenever their diplomats fail. It represents the natural state of the human condition, retreating to the primal instinct of competing with everyone that stands in the way of superiority. Peace, on the other hand, merely provides a colloquial term that matters little without a complete lack of aggression within the world. War, therefore, need not consist of battles and victories, though it often employs them to set limits on endurance or expenditure.

Whenever someone believes that you remain a threat to his or her survival or his or her way of life, war exists. Whenever a group or an organization seeks to profit from your destruction or subjugation, war exists. Whenever someone attacks you or another group with the intent to injure or cause indiscriminate destruction of property, war exists. Thus, we can dispense with the myriad of international laws and regulations; war is what you are confronted with whenever another party forces you into doing what you do not believe in doing. The choice to fight, or not, is entirely up to your discretion.

The presence of an active shooter within your

school or university pits that person's maniacal obsession with his or her grievances against the safety and security of your community.

The presence of a homicide bomber within a crowded congregation places his or her religious beliefs against your own concept of faith and peace.

The presence of a bogus ambulance racing towards the most exposed point of a hospital challenges your ability to provide aid and comfort to the vulnerable.

These are acts of *war*, whether you choose to accept the fact or not. Your participation does not define conflict, as many "neutral" nations during the world wars suffered consequences at the hands of the belligerents. Again, war is not the result of genocide; genocide is the result of war. Accordingly, your community remains at war as soon as a threatening individual or group perceives an attack against it.

This represents the reason why your tactical action plan requires detailed intelligence in order to formulate procedural doctrine. It further explains why considerable effort must be placed into counterintelligence, so that these threats cannot capitalize upon your weaknesses. Defense consists of internal *and* external responsibilities that do not materialize by the clock or through available resources.

Most importantly, war remains *digital*. You are either at war or in peace – nothing "in-between" exists in anyone's language. There remains no peace if someone is activity striking you or passively plotting to do so, for as long as there remains intent to inflict harm, actuality is merely an action away. Unfortunately, intentions are extremely difficult to perceive – even by intelligence professionals (a primary example representing Saddam Hussein's invasion of Kuwait).

Because human activities remain so universal and indiscriminate, very little is conceived of with absolute originality. For example, just because the Wright Brothers were the first to fly a heavy-than-air craft, did not mean that thousands of others were not fabricating methods of doing so too. In fact, gunpowder may represent the very last fully original invention, as no one had conceived of a chemical explosive prior to its emergence.

What this means for your community, is that there exists *examples* of schools being attack (at least as far back as 1927), churches destructed (currently undertaken within the greater Middle East and Northern Africa – MENA), and hospitals suffering acute aggression (everywhere, and for decades). Your particular facility may appear safe and secure, but thousands of its brethren are screaming in horror.

As with any addiction, wars require recognition before society can deal with the disease. In this, the world has been troublingly ineffective. Since the late 1700s, millions of people have been murdered *outside the constraints of declared warfare* and almost exclusively in blocks of hundreds of thousands of victims at a time. The numbers remain so staggering that all but the most isolated researcher can perceive of them. The rest of humanity rolls through life as if a few hundred thousand dead Christians here or a few million dead Jews there matters little.

Contemporary society remains extremely selfish and divisive, despite the best efforts of a few noble individuals. Even the globally expansive, yet actively impotent United Nations *observes* more atrocities than it prevents or terminates. So much for international diplomacy.

Only in boxing, can a battered opponent cast in the towel and retreat to plan for another bout without relinquishing his opportunities or sacrificing his reputation. When war confronts your community, however, the proverbial gloves must come off. There will be *no* "tomorrow" should that gunman, homicide bomber, or explosives-laden ambulance succeed. Could *you* live peacefully if you could have stopped either from happening but chose to flee or submit?

During the early 19th century, Prussian strategist Carl von Clausewitz wrote:

> "Kind-hearted people might of course think there was some ingenious way to disarm or defeat an enemy without too much bloodshed, and might imagine this is the true goal of the art of war. Pleasant as it sounds, this is a fallacy that must be exposed: war is such a dangerous business that the mistakes which come from kindness are the very worst. The maximum use of force is in no way incompatible with the simultaneous use of the intellect."[16]

These words were written well before the invention of the machinegun, nerve gas, atomic weaponry, intercontinental ballistic missiles, airplanes, or, especially, electronic computers and cell phones.

If your community, be it a school or church, is similarly attacked, "kind-hearted people" will likely be

---

[16] Carl von Clausewitz, *On War* ed. and trans. Michael Howard and Peter Paret (Princeton, NJ: Princeton University Press, 1976), 75.

amongst the first casualties. This is primarily because *kindness* is a virtue and not a defense mechanism. During the Holy Wars of Europe during the 17th century, thousands of innocent souls perished because they believed that God would stop cannon shells and bullets. Today, during the 21st century, we *should* know better. Yet, we do not.

Whenever tragedy strikes, as with a school or church shooting, those in power (i.e., acting as if *God*) remain quick to propose new legislation or violate old rights. These legislators are not even acting "kind-hearted", they seek to prove to the world that he or she remains more powerful than human aggression. Where they differ from the aggressors is that the "mad gunmen" of the world remain honest in his or her actions. They *intend* to harm innocent human lives. Politicians and bureaucrats merely *do so*.

When members of your community or facility look you squarely into the eyes and ask, "What are *you* doing to protect us?" will your answer be equally dishonest? Will your entire plan of defense rest on well-typed doctrine rather than well-trained staff? When the wolves come to your door, will you open the gateway for sheep or sheepdogs?

There is no shame in admitting that certain things in life, such as child abuse or animal cruelty, drive you to rage. Anger represents a fundamental human emotion. However, when fear overtakes this rage, even under the delusion of "kind-hearted" action, then only disaster develops. You must channel your primal rage into appropriate action. You must act as if the devoted sheepdog – kind and playful until aroused; and then you sink your fangs into wolves' necks.

You may question the sanity of "behaving like the bad guys" under the sentiment of little separating the two of you, but the fact remains that once you are safe and secure, you *will* go back to your pre-battle routine. This is what separates the naturally aggressive from the naturally protective – your ability to 'turn off' when not threatened. Aggressors *cannot* turn off, no matter how deceptive he or she may be.

You can observe this with a casual glance at the evening news. Watch someone that remains on the defensive about his or her position, whether that involves political or social issues, or, perhaps, coming to the aid of aggressors. This individual will fidget within his or her seat, their eyelids will constrict, and, if you are paying close enough attention, you will see their skin actually change hue. *This particular individual does not believe that he or she actually needs to defend his or her position.*

When you, as a conscientious citizen, engage within discussion amongst your community, if even if at odds with everyone else, you do not feel the need to burst out of your skin to argue your point, now do you? Peek back at Figure 5 again. These individuals on television are not good representatives of his or her position because they are easily riled and this turns most people away from hearing their point of view.

This reality is prevalent within war. During the Battle of Saipan in 1944, hundreds of Japanese mothers launched their children over the cliffs of Marpi Point just before jumping down onto the piling bodies beneath.[17] The reason for this atrocity, which horrified even hardened combat veterans, was that the Japanese government instructed them that in doing so, they would receive the same glory and recognition

---

[17] Thomas J. Cutler, *The Battle of Leyte Gulf: 23-26 October 1944* (Annapolis, MD: Naval Institute Press, 1994), 11.

as that nation's fallen soldiers.[18] In reality, it symbolized that the Japanese citizens preferred to kill even their unborn children rather than fall captive to the Americans. Such fanaticism can only come by way of extreme manipulation on the part of Japanese authority (remember Dr. Milgram's research!), even if that authority rests a great many thousands of miles away from the confrontation.

Of course, surrender to the Americans did not end the lives of *all* Japanese people as that particular nation rose from literal ashes to become an economic powerhouse in a few short decades. What the lesson teaches us here, however, is that *some* people are even willing to kill their children just because they fear our way of life.

As with Kamikaze aircraft crashing into our naval carriers, today's homicide bombers – and even some active shooters – engage upon a last-ditch effort to kill themselves as they seek to kill us. No doubt, the citizens of Saipan remained clueless as to the nature of the United States, but when individuals – as with those hostile interviewees on the television news – seal his or her mind off from opposing thought, they fall trap to radicalism.

Nowhere within modern, "peaceful" society is this refusal to consider opposing thoughts more evident than with those who believe that an individual bears no fundamental right to protect him or herself – especially with firearms.

---

[18] Ibid., 12.

9. WEAPONRY

IF we conclude that, by itself, a "weapon" is merely "Any instrument used in combat" then we must allow that any instrument *may* be used in combat.[19] From here, we can deduce that any instrument *not* employed in combat is not a weapon. This distinction bears merit, for a weapon is an *operator-centric* device whereas the instrument remains a *manufactured object.*

For instance, a butcher knife may be used to slice beef, but can also be used to behead a captive individual. Similarly, a hatchet is designed to split wood, but it can also kill unsuspecting police officers. Conversely, a particular firearm may be used to kill soldiers on a battlefield, but its *designed function* is to transmit cartridges into a chamber and bullets down a barrel. Nothing more; nothing less. To suggest that a 21st century firearm is more or less lethal than an 18th century flintlock amounts to saying that a bronze hatchet is more or less deadly than a modern ax made from carbon steel. After all, Biblical Samson allegedly killed a thousand men with the jawbone of an ass; one

---

[19] *The Grosset Webster Dictionary, New Revised Edition* eds. William Morris, Charles P. Chadsey, and Harold Wentworth (New York: Grosset & Dunlap, 1966). 625, Definition 1.

would not normally consider a bone an instrument of warfare.

Within the context of this book, however, we shall eliminate the hysteria involving weapons. For convenience, we shall limit our broader categorization to those instruments whose lethality requires no modification from the operator and those whose capacity to inflict injury or death anticipates some manner of creativity on the part of that user. For example, the hatchets often used by Native Americans during the colonial phase of our history represent *subconscious* weapons. That is, people generally know what can be done with a sharp blade, for instance.

Samson's jawbone of an ass, to the contrary, represents something of a *conscious* weapon; the Biblical hero had to employ his consciousness in order to use the bone to inflict pain and suffering. By itself, the "instrument" was just a fragment of a donkey's skull. The same process assuredly arose when the first cave dweller decided that the rock that he nearly tripped over made for terminating his neighbor.

Accordingly, when we discuss firearms – rifles, shotguns, and pistols – we will not dwell on the subjective confusion imparted by the frenzy-salivating media. Instead, we will describe all firearms under their legal definition, as outlined above. For example, the AKMS shown in Figure 8 is a rifle with a folding stock (hence, the AKM*S* designation instead of AKM for modernized AK-47). It retains its classification as a rifle due to the rifling in its barrel. That said, because the firearm is 26 inches or less, it is further subcategorized as a *pistol* within the United States, particularly in states such as Michigan where the "pistol" opens up possibilities through licensed concealed or non-licensed open carry.

Others, especially the media, attempt to classify the AKM/AKMS as an "assault weapon" insofar as militaries *may* use the firearm (rather, its fully automatic version) during raids and ambushes. This merely adds a personification to an inanimate object, such as declaring high-horsepower automobiles from the 1960s as "muscle cars".

Figure 8. AKMS rifle in 7.62 x 39mm caliber. © R.J. Godlewski

From the technical perspective, firearms are categorized in terms of caliber of bullet (in fractions of an inch or millimeters) and length of cartridge (almost exclusively listened in metric). For example, the AKMS shown in Figure 8 employs the standard "AK-47" round of 7.62 x 39 mm. Figure 9 offers a size comparison of several popular rounds. Figure 10 depicts what is traditionally referred to as a *battle rifle* – meaning that it fires a full-sized rifle cartridge (in this instance, 7.62 x 51 mm, employing the same size of bullet as the AKM, but using a longer casing).

To complicate the news media even further,

most "assault rifle" rounds are not specifically designed to *kill*; rather, they are intended to injure so that militaries must expend personnel transporting wounded soldiers to safety. In theory, that is.

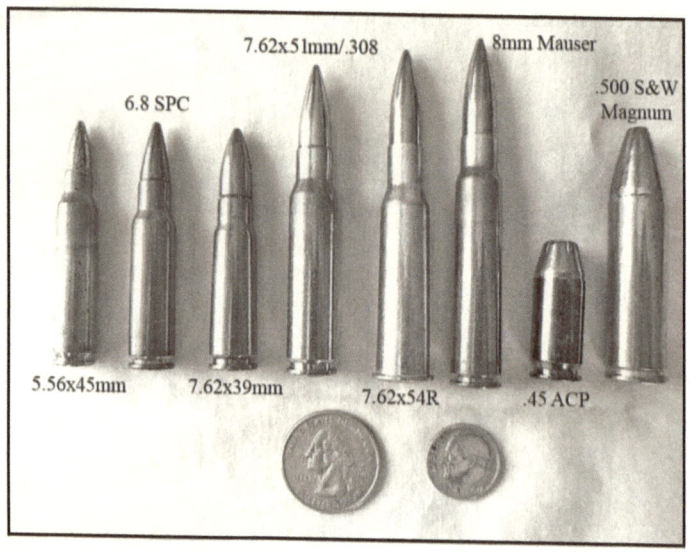

Figure 9. Cartridge comparisons. (L-R), 5.56 x 45mm, 6.8mm SPC, 7.62 x 39mm, 7.62 x 51mm [.308], 7.62 x 54R, 8mm Mauser, .45 ACP, and .500 S&W Magnum. © R.J. Godlewski

In contrast, most full-sized rifle cartridges, many developed for hunting large animals, *are* designed to be lethal. These include such cartridges as the 7.62 x 51mm NATO (the U.S. .308 caliber), the 7.62 x 54R (a 'rimmed' cartridge used by the Soviet Mosin-Nagant rifle in World War II), and the 8mm Mauser used in German-developed Mauser action rifles. Incidentally, the latter two rifles are *bolt-action* rifles, as are most hunting rifles, and each round must be manually racked into the chamber by the shooter. In *semi-automatic* firearms, as with all pistols except revolvers, the action of the gun, usually through use of the expanding gas of discharge, chambers the next round automatically.

Fully automatic weapons, wherein the gun shoots continuously as long as the trigger is depressed, are extremely rare even within the United States. Those that do exist are pre-1986 collector's items, costing several tens of thousands of dollars, or illicit firearms used exclusively by criminal gangs.

Figure 10. PTR-91-KFM4 battle rifle in 7.62 x 51mm NATO. © R.J. Godlewski

Another consideration involves the very nature of the firearm's bullet itself, which could be a full-metal jacket (FMJ) bullet used by all military as per international agreement, or one of numerous types of expanding bullets (usually of the 'hollow point' variety) used in personal defense situations where aggressors need to be stopped quickly. Incidentally, beware of the anti-gun argument that large-capacity magazines are somehow "evil". The human body, particularly one animated by a drug-influenced mind, can withstand considerable damage before the individual is finally incapacitated. Politicians may seek to restrict the number of bullets a person carries, but the "law of the jungle" mandates that more is better.

Comparative Bullet Diameters

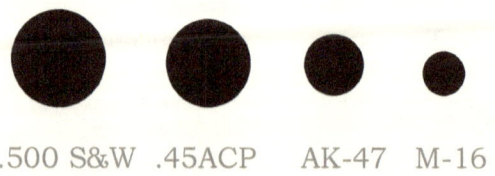

.500 S&W   .45ACP   AK-47   M-16

Figure 11. DPMS/Panther Arms AP-4 in 5.56x45mm. Comparative bullet sizes. © R.J. Godlewski

In Figure 11, we see a civilian version of the M-4 carbine (consider it a "modernized" version of the AR-15/M-16 family). Aside from the Kalashnikov AK-47/AKM firearms, this American "assault rifle" is the most maligned gun in history. Nevertheless, its 5.56mm/.223 bullet is amongst the *smallest* of all global firearms (see Figure 11, top). This exemplifies the hysteria caused by those ignorant of firearms and their design, confirming that those opposed to firearms ownership want *all* guns out of citizens' hands rather than an allegedly few "military weapons"

Figure 12. Ruger SR-556 in 6.8 SPC. © R.J. Godlewski

Even a casual glance at Figure 12 suggest a far more "militarized" firearm than the M-4 clone in Figure 11, but the Ruger SR-556, in this 6.8 SPC cartridge (nearly the same bullet as in the .270 cartridge) configuration, *is* a legitimate hunting round. This illustration proves that the firearm "package" is deceiving; the uninitiated may conclude that military firearms and "sporting" firearms are distinct types. They are not as the vast majority of firearms used in military history have come from hunting versions.

The scope, bipod, and sling depicted in Figure 12 remain relatively low-cost (compared with other accessories) *add-ons* to make the firearm more controllable by its owner, who, incidentally, suffers from arthritis. These accessories could be affixed to the battle rifle in Figure 10 and its function would not change any. In fact, for the PTR91KFM4 to serve better as a *hunting* rifle, such additions would be expected.

With this discussion passed, we can return to understanding weaponry as it applies to your particular community. Firearms merely represent a small portion of the threats against your facility, but they *may* serve admirably in the protection of that location, which we shall discuss in subsequent chapters. For now, we need to consider all weaponized threats.

To focus your mind more on reality than hyperbole, it must be remembered that perpetrators bearing box cutters that virtually anyone can locate at their neighborhood store carried out the greatest terrorist attack in U.S. history – the September 11, 2001 attacks against Washington, D.C. and New York City. Remember, also, that the worst school massacre in U.S. history did not involve "assault rifles" or firearms of any kind; the Bath, Michigan disaster of 1927 resulted from a disgruntled resident filling his old truck with dynamite and rusty machinery parts.

No matter *what* communities ban, *someone* will locate another instrument of war to carry the battle onto your doorstep. From hatchets to machetes to automobiles, people will find a way of targeting your vulnerabilities in order to inflict the worst possible damage. The less able you are to defend, the easier it is for them to attack.

Criminals are also fundamentally aware of the concept of *improvised weaponry* – the reuse of any implement to strike at the exceptionally frail human body. From pipes to broom handles to frying pans and on to umbrella spikes, *anything* that strikes against or penetrates the human body can lead to extreme damage.

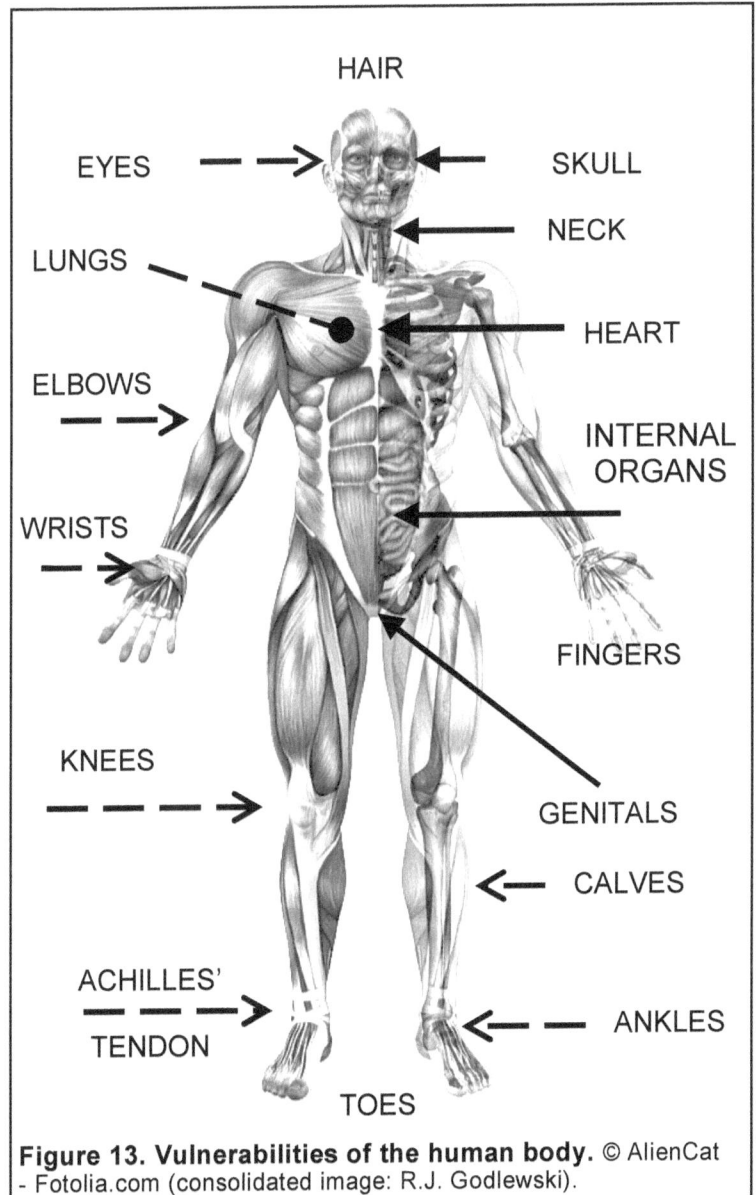

Figure 13. Vulnerabilities of the human body. © AlienCat - Fotolia.com (consolidated image: R.J. Godlewski).

The criminal use of such improvised weapons results from, generally, the inability of that individual for legally obtaining any other weapons. Others, such as long-haul truckers, keep devices such as beef hooks (for suspending frozen carcasses) for defense since company rules or local laws prevent them from carrying firearms for protection. It is odd that others, particularly in "soft targets", are not familiar with the use of so-called everyday objects for defense against attack.

In Figure 13, we observe the vulnerabilities of the human body. Any of the muscles, bones, and organs can be damaged with the slightest effort. To impart this damage, one needs only to strike, stomp, kick, gouge, bite, or throw – actions not requiring *any* external object whatsoever. With a pencil, pen, car key, umbrella, cane, or any other small cylindrical object, one can also poke, stab, and slice. Larger objects, such as fire extinguishers, chairs, books, frying pans, briefcases, etc. may be used to severely bruise large muscles and shatter smaller bones when pinned against solid objects.

Since the mere act of walking implies an imbalance of an individual's center of gravity, *any* effort to disrupt an assailant's balance – through unarmed or improvised tactics – provides the defender with many additional options. For instance, a quick strike with a briefcase can send a disoriented mugger down a flight of stairs, leading to significant injuries in the process. Alternately, a swing at an attacker's knees from the back will cause them to drop, which should then be followed up with a two-handed back swing at the neck. In most cases, these two quick actions will incapacitate all but the strongest and most fleet-footed individual.

Now that the reader is versed in improvised weaponry – to a very basic degree – he or she must move to perceive defenses against these attacks in case the tables are turned on the use of such weapons. Even with the example of an active shooter, he or she may employ non-firearm weapons should you or any of your staff foil their attempt to shoot his or her way into the history books. This requires you to condition yourself to protect those vital areas outlined in Figure 13.

The basic stance towards defending oneself against *any* attack is to pivot so that your body is turned laterally towards the attacker. This provides him or her with a narrower target to focus upon. It also means that most of your vital areas are protected by a deeper cross-section. Furthermore, most individuals find it easier to bend forward or backward than towards the left or right. What this means is that if, for instance, you face your left side towards the attacker, you will be able to dip forward or bend backwards to deflect oncoming attacks. By remaining in a frontal position, turning towards either side – or even ducking – will not remove much of your body mass from the attacker's perspective.

In this regard, you should note that this is the preferred stance of baseball pitchers as they are able to generate more thrust towards the plate than if he were standing parallel to the first baseman. If the attacker were to strike at the back of your knees in order to incapacitate you, this position further allows you to fall backwards, reducing any danger from any follow-through from the assailant. In other words, if the attacker is right-handed, he is likely to swing his right leg at your knees. In this situation, face your *left side* against him and should he reach your legs, you will fall *backwards* – towards his right – and away from any simultaneous strikes.

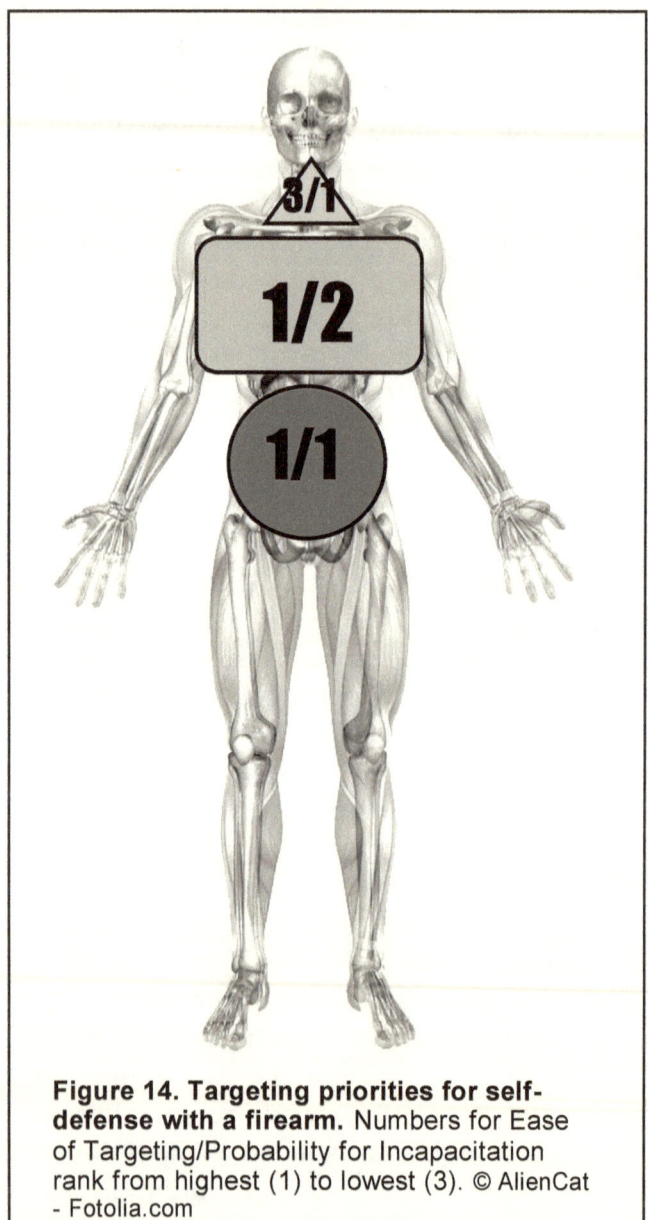

Figure 14. Targeting priorities for self-defense with a firearm. Numbers for Ease of Targeting/Probability for Incapacitation rank from highest (1) to lowest (3). © AlienCat - Fotolia.com

While improvised weapons are capable of defending your life or that of other members of your community, they are, just that, weapons *improvised* because none other exist. They are, in essence, a *last ditch option* taken under the premise that, despite catcalls from the martial arts community, bare hands make for horrible weapons. What you need remains a weapon made of steel and, herein, we return to the proud firearm.

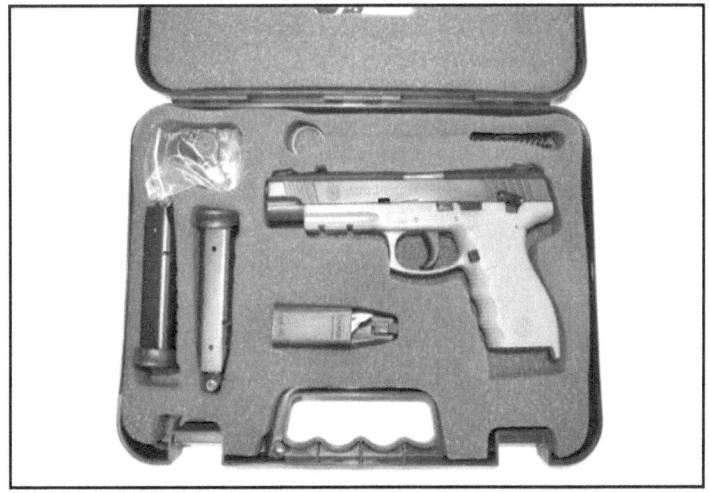

Figure 15. Taurus 24/7 in .45 ACP caliber. Firearm (circa 2008) since replaced by improved versions. © R.J. Godlewski.

In Figure 15, we observe an example of an ideal self-defense firearm – the (now superseded) Taurus 24/7 OSS in .45 ACP. This light, ergonomic semi-automatic pistol carries 12 rounds in each of its magazines, and one in the chamber for a grand total of 13 rounds of ammunition before a quick change towards another magazine is required. The Taurus 24/7 family was designed for the military special operations community and are capable of reliable firing throughout any climate or environment.

Carried, say, in the small of the back with an IWB (inside the waistband) holster, this rather large firearm is very concealable by any normal-sized man with little more than a loose tee shirt. In a matter of seconds, a trained shooter can stop any aggressor before they cover the "safety zone" separating the two individuals. With smaller caliber firearms – of the .38 Special and even 9mm variety – the odds for surviving an onrush are quite limited as was observed by the U.S. military fighting Moro tribesmen in early 20th century Philippines.

The reason that your community must adopt firearms use is that *all other weapons for defense* prove ineffective. The same could be said with the wide variety of caliber and ammunition options available. Your people require the largest cartridge that they can safely – and *accurately* – shoot. Frangible rounds – such as the 5.56mm cartridge depicted in Figure 9 – disintegrate upon striking dense materials. This keeps them from ricocheting off doors and other hard objects. They come in many pistol and rifle calibers.

Regardless of which firearm or ammunition that your community chooses, anyone targeting an aggressor *must fire continually until his or her attacker is demonstrably unable to inflict harm*. This may mean discharging all 12 rounds of a comparable firearm before you can rest assured that the perpetrator will not cause you or other innocent parties harm. Only unqualified political pundits with an agenda declare that there is no need to fire more than one or two rounds at an attacker.

In Figure 14, we see the three vital areas of a human figure and their respective ease of targeting and probability for incapacitation. You will immediately note two observations. First, one must shoot at the largest body mass available. Second, these opportunistic targets still contain a great many voids where even passing bullets may not inflict any harm upon the attacker.

Figure 16. The most powerful production revolver on the planet: the Smith & Wesson .500 Magnum. © R.J. Godlewski.

In a real world scenario, such as if two street thugs were trying to rape your teenage daughter, then primal human survivability would want you to bear a "*Handgun for any ... animal walking*" (See Figure 16).[20] However, even in such a horrific setting, there is such a thing as 'over kill' and despite your honest desire for possessing a "hand cannon", you have to employ more practical firearms in your community's defense.

Yet, what *if* your situation warranted something with power (as in Figure 15), a greater ammunition

___

[20] http://www.smith-wesson.com. Accessed October, 2015.

capability (as in Figures 11 and 12), but long guns as a rifle or a shotgun were not convenient (say, if you had to deal with tight corridors or confined spaces)?

With considerable research and testing on your part, you may want to evaluate a firearm such as the Masterpiece Arms MPA-10T in .45 ACP caliber (see Figure 17). This stocky firearm – perhaps too big to conceal within a shoulder holster – employs 30-round magazines, two additional ones easily contained on the opposite side of a tactical shoulder harness. This provides your community's defense team up to ninety rounds per individual – ammunition that can take the shape of virtually any configuration, including frangible and fragmentation rounds.

Figure 17. Masterpiece Arms MPA-10T in .45 ACP. Shown with 30-round magazine and optional barrel extension (for ease in handling). © R.J. Godlewski

While some – if not most – people may consider firearms such as the MPA-10T slightly "drastic", the pistol offers several advantages over, say, rifles of the M-4 variety. First, without a barrel extension, its total length reduces to a manageable 10.5 inches (~26 cm).

This means that security personnel can carry the firearm around without panicking other members of your community. Second, its cost is approximately one-quarter that of tactical rifles. Economically speaking, your community would be able to protect four times the real estate or four times the number of classrooms for the same expense to your program. Finally, the larger, slower moving bullet will do a far better job of stopping aggressors, especially if you have to shoot through windows or other climatic disturbances.

Careful consideration of both firearm type and caliber size must be at the forefront of your decision to include firearms into your defensive perimeter. First, you must intimately understand just how bullets kill:

Wound Ballistics[21]

The primary property of a modern bullet in flight remains its velocity and its stability as affected by the spin imparted upon it from the rifling within the firearm's barrel. In this environment, the bullet rests within its realm and will carry on through its trajectory towards the ground under the auspices of gravity *unless* it impacts against an intruding target, wherein it either comes to an abrupt halt or ricochets.

When a bullet strikes human tissue – at roughly 800 to 900 times denser than air[22] – it immediately destabilizes and begins to tumble releasing its energy and causing injury in three ways (assuming that it did not represent a *powerful enough* bullet that it would pass

---

[21] This section reprinted from R.J. Godlewski, *Mini-Manual of the Independent Counterterrorist, Third Edition* (Charleston, SC: CreateSpace Independent Publishing Platform, 2014), 120-122.

through the body). The first represents the cutting and crushing of tissue as the bullet initially enters into the body. The second mechanism involves the shock wave produced by supersonic bullets; this travels outwards at the speed of sound within water – 4,800 feet per second.[23]

The third injury causing mechanism represents *temporary cavitation*. The bullet forces energy outward and *forward* when it enters the body, even producing momentum for long after the bullet has finally exited the victim. This energy release causes the formation of the large cavity that essentially consists of the wound track and may be upwards of *thirty times* the bullet diameter.[24] This effect remains so violent that it may destroy capillaries far removed from the actual path of the bullet.

Perhaps, it would behoove us to examine things from a different perspective. Let us take a less technical view of the 5.56mm AR-15 round. At distances of less than 100 yards, it is traveling at nearly three thousand feet per second when it strikes against the human body. The bullet, being small and unstable now, begins to tumble at, perhaps, ninety degrees before it reaches a full four inches into the body and begins to disintegrate into smaller fragments.[25] What had just been traveling at greater than the speed of sound – as if a military jet fighter on full afterburner – *stops* in a matter of a few inches. All that powerful momentum has to go *somewhere* and that somewhere represents the body's tissues, bones, and blood vessels.

What was once healthy living 'body' now remains a conduit for a supersonic shockwave traveling up virtually every blood vessel, through every cell, and reverberating within every fluid within your body. They

---

[22] Adrian Gilbert, *Sniper: One on One: The World of Combat Sniping* (London: Sidgwick & Jackson, 1994), 124.
[23] Ibid., 125.
[24] Ibid., 126.
[25] Ibid., 129.

literally explode until the energy is ultimately dissipated. I will spare you the rest, but just remember the effects of the slight "shock" of, say, your leg when it hits the ground a bit too hard. Now imagine that shock amplified thousands of times.

The human body is *not* rigid like a mannequin. It is mostly fluid with relatively few bones to keep the fluids and soft tissue into shape. What one part of your body experiences, the others share to a degree (we learned this through cross training). Therefore, a bullet hitting a human body (or animal body for that matter) does not simply "drill" a hole through a solid object. It *pierces a fluid object* and the resulting shock waves literally vaporize anything that is not solid. Should this "fluid object" represent, say, the human brain, then the resulting damage magnifies exponentially as untold millions of electrical impulses shoot throughout the body *instantaneously*. Chickens are *not* the only animals that can briefly scurry around without heads attached.

These three mechanisms for wound generation represent the effectiveness of the firearm over nearly all other handheld weapons. They also represent what sends shivers up the spine of rational human beings. This realization merely underscores the importance of *training* when dealing with firearms in *any* capacity. Again, the right to self-defense represents a "grave duty" and this is for a very good reason.

Unlike your adversaries that seek to harm and kill as many people as they can – almost exclusively anticipating death on his or her own part – *your* function remains to stop the aggressor while *saving* lives. Yet, you *will* be accorded the same treatment once the shooting ceases. That is, despite the number of lives you or your staff save, politics and common public reaction will mandate that you suffer the consequences in court.

There remain several reasons for this. The most obvious one deals with the loss of lives, even if only the aggressor's. We live within a very litigious society where *everyone* eventually finds an attorney and, yes, the person who intended to kill children in a school or patients in a hospital will be defended by his or her next of kin as if a hero. They will seek damages for your "rendering the aggressor unable to inflict harm."

The second reason is that once things settle down a bit, the public will have a reaction to the news that someone other than legitimate public authority had to act with extreme prejudice. A great many will support you, yes, but *every* individual or organization bears its share of enemies. These critics will push legislators to accommodate some new law that will take what you just accomplished and place it back into the hands of bureaucratic authority. This *reaction* will simmer for years afterwards.

The final reason that you will suffer in court is that most of the world remains populated by sheep, people largely incapable of responding to *any* crisis with determination. These individuals represent those who "flee" or "submit" rather than even posture. That you chose to *fight* rather than die, automatically labels you as a "killer". You (or your community) will have blood on its hands and, frankly, such heroes only appear within the movies and on television. In society, they remain outcasts. Your appearance in court only grants them a chance to terminate your employment without aggravating those whom you saved.

10. DAMAGE CONTROL

BEFORE we break into individual discussion regarding various scenarios involving schools, churches, hospitals, etc., we must ensure that you understand what it is that you are about to undertake. Thus far, this book took you through various independent phases that, when combined, lead to the concept of self-preservation and defense for your community, regardless of how small that organization is. And, yes, we have considered wherever you work, or teach, or preach as a bona fide *community*.

Human beings remain social creatures, as long as there are two together; we bond as a community unit. That is, once we finally abandon the competitive/aggressive phase that serves little more than to observe others with suspicion. Nevertheless, in all communities, no matter how tiny – consider Cain and Abel, for instance – there will be individuals that want to harm and murder for no "apparent" reason. His or her grievances will run the gamut and studied for decades with little to add. Some people are just plain *evil*.

If you are reading this book, however, you believe that all people are fundamentally good and, for this very reason, you want to do *something* should the need to survive ever affect your particular community.

This is admirable. If more people were as dedicated to saving human lives, even if only his or her own, there would be far less atrocities within the world. Unfortunately, because you represent such a kind and compassionate individual, active defense *will* forever change your entire life. Whatever the future holds, you will *not* emerge as someone recognizable to the soul reading these words today.

A few military writers have told stories regarding decent young men going through what is termed "shock training" only to emerge with the ability to slit throats with ease. Yet, these represent warriors in soldier's clothing. At best, you will represent a warrior in sheep's clothing. At worst, a Chihuahua in a Rottweiler's coat. It will take a great many years to transform the "kind-hearted" into the aggressive unless total shock immersion is endured. Chances are that you will not possess ex-Navy SEALs or former Delta Force commandos on your staff. And, frankly, you do not need them.

If your community possessed the need for hardened military operatives, then, perhaps, you have already *lost* the war thrust upon you by those who want to rattle your life forever. Nevertheless, kindling that "warrior" within your soul may do much to serve your future regardless of external responsibilities. To represent a *warrior* does not mean that you engage within combat or warfare exclusively. What being a warrior means, quite literally, is that you undertake everything not as a hobby, but as an integral part of your life; that self-defense and protection represent a *calling*, rather than a pastime; and that you devote every available moment to the perfection of your inner character and not wasteful leisure activities.[26]

Being a warrior does not mean that you must abandon your family, your friends, or that tee on the back nine. Rather, that whenever you remain with your family, visit your friends, or engage within any pleasurable pursuit, that you *focus* intimately on the task. No wasteful thoughts, no daydreaming and fantasies – *every thought you possess* rests squarely upon the effort or question before you.

This is not exceedingly difficult, but for most people, they cannot walk and talk at the same time. Nor can they drive without having his or her cell phone glued to their ears. The *slightest* distraction may cost you your life. This retreats to that, "Gosh, officer, I did not see that deer coming!" mentality that afflicts motorists all over the countryside. *Why* did they not see a 200-pound animal rushing through the thickets? Could they *not* see the commotion of the moving animal? The scurrying of birds? That DEER CROSSING sign alongside the road?

People generally do not pay attention to his or her surroundings, a fact alleged on a documentary television show where a person interviewed a shopper about a rather innocuous subject. Briefly, they were somewhat rudely "interrupted" as two men passed between them carrying a large sheet of plywood. The interview continued – with one slight difference. The person originally speaking to the shopper took the position of the individual holding the rear of the plywood and he, in turn, took over the microphone to interview the shopper. Strangely, the several

[26] Forrest E. Morgan, *Living the Martial Way: A Manual for the Way a Modern Warrior Should Think* (Fort Lee, NJ: Barricade Books, 1992), 17-31.

interviewees *never* caught the difference.

For what it is worth, this tale suggests that few people can pay close enough attention to details to pick out the identity of someone standing directly in front of him or her. As a society, we remain so absorbed within ourselves that we fail to identify the uniqueness within every single preson (see Chapter 2). You *must* observe details if you are going to protect your interests following an attack upon your community. The authorities, the media, the public, *everyone* will scour your words and deeds for any hint that you did not understand what you were getting into.

Fortunately, humans do not retain sufficient memory within the immediate aftermath of a crisis to be of much use to the authorities – assuming that you are not a conditioned high-risk professional. This means that if you are involved within a shooting, for instance, *avoid* making any statements to the police. Kindly tell them that you would be glad to speak to them about the incident – after you have conversed with your attorney – after a couple of days. Unless your expedient information were useful in saving lives or apprehending criminals on the loose, simply do not compromise yourself through making rash statements.

Very few people possess sufficient memory recall in normal situations; what you are planning for – and, undoubtedly, vocally praying that you *never* witness – represents a crime of such magnitude that you will likely be in shock for these several days. Your world, as teacher, preacher, or healer, is not prepared for just such contingencies. As a product of either public or private schools, the modern trend rests towards tolerance and acceptance; community and collective. No one is teaching you how to deal with competition – *let alone aggression.*

Survival – *after the fact* – rests squarely upon your shoulders. You will become a pariah to some, a nuisance to others. Few will always remain appreciative (usually those whose lives were directly saved, and even they may renege if the opportunity arises). Your community, if not your name, will become a footnote in history leaving future historians to wonder whatever happened within your heretofore-peaceful population.

Ours represents an entirely *packaged* society. We judge our products based upon how appealing they are, how marketable they are, and whether they will instill envy upon others. As such, we criticize everything. We condemn books for being too easy or hard to read, too thick or too thin, and whether they appeared as the result of a bureaucracy or a mere individual's effort. We pitch companies as environmentally or socially sound and promote our politicians as belonging to the "correct" ideology. Lastly, we scan for the latest rankings of our college football teams even though the season has yet to begin.

Everything that we do or strive for has to remain *approved* by others that neglect our best interests. Therefore, whenever your particular community arises from a chaotic situation, few will care whether you did what you believed was right or that you saved a great many people. They will look at the *image* of what you did and mirror image that action upon what *they* would have done within your situation. As if it really matters.

By now, you have run through the prerequisites of understanding human value and its need for survival. You evaluated the concepts of defense and its martial underpinnings. You have analyzed your personnel requirements, and how intelligence and counterintelligence may provide them with tactical advantage over perceived threats. You have even acquiesced to the notion of *war* and entertained a few of the instruments used to affect it. Now, however, you are questioning the sanity of it all.

This is merely routine and quite normal amongst the human species. We represent the only creatures on earth that seek to annihilate ourselves out of existence. If this were not the case, people would not be as adamant about keeping your safety in the hands of others. Your seeming violation of *their* rules will only serve to aggravate them even further. Of course, you would not have it any other way.

You are reading this book because you are seeking every tidbit of knowledge that may aid your community in surviving – *not* because it has been packaged properly. This search resulted because the advice out there remains inadequate for your particular community. The continued targeting of similar communities merely because they represent "soft targets" for the taking also deeply saddens you.

Because of this, your "damage control" efforts must exist in three distinct phases: preventative, responsive, and rehabilitative depending upon whether the activity occurs before, during, or following an attack against your community. These efforts will guide you through the various scenarios and effects that your community will likely incur as the result of your scenario proceeding through passive and active measures.

As no two communities are the same, these suggestions will serve as guidelines for your particular case, laying the foundation for your subsequent research. You will need too, of course, the advice of responsible legal representation.

Effective Damage Control

Preventative:

- Your security plan must remain detailed enough to cover every conceivable procedure that your community may have to endure, whether it is a school, university, hospital, church, synagogue, mosque, etc. _Any_ activity that you or your personnel undertake must be addressed within this plan, or, at a minimum, sufficient guidelines exist to grant your team support should "innovation" occur.

- Every minute of training for your staff, whether formal or independent, must be recorded and categorized according to subject, procedural policy affected, and license or credential earned (if any). This training must cover equipment, tactics, first aid, and liability issues regarding the aforementioned.

- Your defense and security plan must involve law enforcement and other emergency response agencies within your training and procedural writing. They need not, however, know of information that you do not wish to be shared with outside parties, but their involvement overall should be substantial enough that "surprises" do not occur.

- The public – insofar as practical – should be made

knowledgeable of your commitment (if not procedures) to protect your community. Without disclosing proprietary information, certain elements of your program must be made available so that students, parishioners, patients, etc. – individuals that may possess a very transitory perception of your particular environment – will not become barriers whenever elements of your plan are enacted.

Responsive:

- Whenever an emergency occurs – whether an active shooter, terrorist attack, disgruntled employee, or simply fire – the *first* action that your staff should undertake remains to direct innocent parties *out* of your facility and into the closest securable zone. You will "barricade" *only* when safe egress is not possible, such as when people would be forced to head *into* the presence of the danger. Otherwise, the order of the day should be *continual movement* towards safety.

- Ancillary staff not immediately aiding in the safety of others, should begin to record the conditions and environment of their surroundings, preferably with cameras. He or she should take note of any messages or broadcasts received from the facility or institution, the presence of other individuals, and the actions taken by those persons within the immediate vicinity. This information will be shared with other staff and, ultimately, the appropriate authorities.

- Insofar as practical, staff should only carry out

those duties and functions outlined within the community's procedural manner. Any deviations from this protocol should be *undertaken solely for the preservation of lives*, even if property may be damaged within the execution of this action. Any accompanying individuals should witness the activity and made aware of the reason for the action.

Rehabilitative:

- As soon as a crisis is over and all members of the security defense team are accounted for, they should meet with the community's leadership at a predetermined location, away from the crisis scene or congregating authorities and/or bystanders.

- Do *not* speak with any law enforcement, investigative, or public officials for a minimum of 24-hours. *Politely* notify all law enforcement authorities that your personnel will make full statements within 24 hours, but they will *not* make any comments until after they have spoken with personal and/or institutional attorneys. If your staff holds information that may aid in the ongoing search for perpetrators, then *that* information may be disclosed – but solely through or in the presence of your security team's senior management.

- Do *not* allow police to inspect personal vehicles, homes, or other properties belonging to members of your team until such activities have been cleared by appropriate legal staff.

- Do not permit individuals within your community

to speak to the media, hold press conferences, or offer any impromptu statements for a period of at least 48 hours *after all active functions have completed.* No information – written, oral, or electronic – should be released while the incident remains an "active news story".

The primary function of damage control functions remains to mitigate liability in the case of a major incident occurring at your facility or involving your personnel. Such information should be contained within your tactical plans' procedural section and communicated to all parties concerned. The transition from preventative to responsive to rehabilitative should ensure that no "surprises" appear that will turn either the local authorities or the public against your best-laid intentions.

Relative *openness*, to the contrary, diminishes through the incident cycle to ensure that no compromising statements are made either to the police or to the public. This is to ensure that your people are not adversely criticized or traumatized by the events for which your plan serves to avoid: innocent deaths and casualties.

11. SOFT TARGETS GALORE

WITHIN any open and civilized democracy, there remains a virtual world of defenseless facilities and locations available for aggressive individuals and organizations to target at will. To harden society against these perpetrators simply extinguishes the libertarian communities that we love and cherish. Nevertheless, the strengthening of *individual* locations and organizations is *not* an affront to free market democracies, rather, the initiative shown by the conscientious citizen concerned about his or her fellow patriots remains the foundation of such freedoms.

Only when we abdicate to political authority exclusively do citizens fear the destruction of his or her freedom and chosen way of life. That is, only when we sacrifice personal responsibility and enterprise for the perceived security of entitlement, does society become less valuable and freedom less sustainable.

As a Western democracy, our way of life rests upon employing taxpayer-funded services as a means to supplement, not replace, our individual contributions and resources. Sadly, because there are always those individuals that cannot – or will not – expend personal effort to succeed, society appears less homogenous than ideally sought. This produces isolated enclaves where "government" has to address the iniquities of social depression – the congregation of people whose isolation fosters resentment towards individualism or success. This, in turn, breeds tribalism of the kind that creates street gangs, narcotics dependency, and groupthink.

Confronting these pockets of anti-social individuals rests, nationwide within the United States, approximately 698,460 total sworn peace officers (against a population of 293,058,940 residents).[27] This translates to about one law enforcement officer per 420 residents in America. If Dr. Milgram's Yale University studies in the 1960s hold true – as subsequent research suggests – then each patrol or beat officer in the U.S. confronts a *potential* of 273 individuals *capable* of inflicting deadly harm upon any one of the other 419 residents of the country.

Viewed from another perspective, each *criminal* that consciously undertakes an aggressive action against his or her neighbor bears only a 1-in-420 chance of encountering a police officer. You, to the contrary, bear an almost 7-in-10 chance of confronting an individual capable of ending your life, or at least seriously injuring it, if we acknowledge the "65% Rule" established by Dr. Milgram.

Further aggravating this scenario, the average response time for these limited police officers ranges from fifteen minutes for smaller communities upwards to forty-five minutes in larger, resource-sapped cities such as Detroit. If an aggressor can subdue existing security measures in less than five minutes that leaves a full ten to forty minutes for them to do as he or she pleases before help arrives.

---

[27] U.S. Federal Bureau of Investigation (2011) statistics.

For this reason, if for no other, facilities such as schools, colleges and universities, hospitals, religious buildings, and other commercial centers such as shopping malls represent *soft* targets. This means that criminals may attack these targets with little threat from responders. This reality exists because:

1. Educational institutions, healthcare facilities, and religious buildings tend to be "gun free" zones;

2. As societal establishments, these facilities represent entities where people go to receive enlightenment or healing, rather than conflict. Therefore, Westerners tend to dismiss the notion that these locations may be dangerous.

3. As public institutions, these facilities draw large groups of individuals into their ranks, swelling both the population of members as well as visitors.

4. Because of the aforementioned flow of personnel, all these facilities are located near major thoroughfares or other transportation nodes.

Taken in unison, these conditions offer to define the "soft target" – an accessible, defenseless facility with large concentrations of vulnerable people.

To defend against aggressors, these facilities require far more than just eliminating one of these conditions. For example, simply permitting citizens to carry firearms may alleviate casualties, but they may *not* deter criminals from attacking (such as if one bears a suicide wish). Similarly, merely locating these properties away from highways, railroad stations, and airports will only sway legitimate visitors from arriving. To secure these varied facilities requires a concerted effort to provide a *unified* defense program. Otherwise, criminals and other dangerous individuals will simply capitalize upon your weakest points.

To secure a facility requires those responsible for it to equalize its defenses. In other words, whereas one may not be able to secure the property completely, the fewer vulnerabilities that remain, the less likely an opportunistic criminal will target that particular facility. Since you may not know what criminals and terrorists specifically target, you must cover all bases and trust that your efforts will dissuade them from eyeing your particular property.

Some of these conditions, such as the number of transient individuals on your property, could not be altered without affecting your institution's purpose. Similarly, relocating a massive university so that it rests away from highways and bus depots cannot even be considered. The other issues *may* increase security through permitting citizens to bear firearms and/or teaching the population that criminals target *all* facilities, including those where people go to encounter God or healing.

Remember, your community facility is *not* a prison or governmental facility. Razor wire fences and roving German shepherds will do little to earn the appreciation of parishioners or patients, even if some schools should be run as if penitentiaries. Any semblances to a top-secret military installation will not only draw the attention of threatening criminals, it will not ingratiate you to your local residents. Your community must appear as if a sound public environment, yet still offer enough protection and "posturing" to ensure that would-be malcontents keep shopping for targets elsewhere.

To begin the process of hardening your community environment, whether it represents a church or a hospital, you must begin to gaze upon it as would a thief or terrorist. This concept, called *red teaming*, uses "friendly" personnel to imitate the bad people that you are *likely* to encounter. This requires professionalism and an intimate knowledge (actionable intelligence) of terrorist and criminal methods and ideologies.

Many law enforcement agencies fail miserably at red team exercises, largely due to his or her inherent "personal biases and love of country" versus an enemy "vehemently disliked and loathed by military and law enforcement personnel".[28] This inability to envision threats from an adversary's perspective is so powerful, that it will be discussed within a separate chapter (See Chapter 12).

For now, we simply need to focus upon why there remain so many soft targets. As discussed, a "soft target" represents any concentration of unarmed people easily accessible to criminals or criminally intent individuals relatively isolated from adequate law enforcement response. Yet, this latter condition remains somewhat misleading: most universities and colleges possess their own police force.

Nevertheless, with the national statistics mentioned earlier within this chapter, even a major university of some 50,000 students is likely to possess fewer than 120 police officers. Dividing this among shifts suggests that fewer than 40 police officers are

---

[28] Stephen Sloan and Robert J. Bunker, *Red Teams and Counterterrorism Training* (Norman, OK: University of Oklahoma Press, 2011), 73.

available to handle any particular emergency. However, even statistics remain misleading.

Arizona State University, with a student population of, perhaps, slightly more than 60,000, retains a police force of less than 87 officers – serving a department with severe staffing and reputational problems.[29] This number translates into 690 students per officer, or about 29 officers per shift, leading concern citizens to question the reasoning behind that particular department's troubles.

Hospitals, for their role, remain even more constricted with only federal institutions and a comparably few states requiring healthcare security operations to be managed by sworn officers. More often than not, healthcare security represents unarmed personnel almost exclusively checking identification badges.

Religious facilities such as churches, synagogues, mosques, etc., represent the proverbial "runt" of the litter, possessing no sworn officers or security personnel in employment. Few even provide physical security systems such as cameras, motion detectors, or keypad entry devices.

The common denominator of soft targets is that they are generally manufactured by the ignorance of those that staff or found them; soft targets thus remain an artificial manifestation.

---

[29] http://www.azcentral.com/story/news/local/tempe/2014/10/31/asu-interim-chief-head-campus-police-force/18263117/

12. RED TEAM ANALYSES

THERE will come a point when *someone* envisions an attack against your community that hardly anyone had considered before. Your facility, in that particular case, may become the "singular" event about which a great many textbooks emerge. Time may dilute the consequences of this attack, as it had with the May 18, 1927 massacre in Bath, Michigan. Or else, as with such incidents as the 2002 Moscow Theater and 2004 Beslan school sieges, live on in infamy.

One hundred years ago, no one could imagine an angry ex-bureaucrat loading his truck with machinery parts and dynamite to blow up a school any more than he or she could have imagined a group of dedicated terrorists threatening to wipe out an entire theater or school full of innocent souls. Conversely, today, few care to remember a time when Native Americans would pepper *wounded* soldiers "full with arrows and chop them in the face with hatchets."[30]

As individuals become more introverted and susceptible to the conveniences of modern society, he or she retains less of the primal human nature that serves to remind us that "such things" *always*

---

[30] Thomas Goodrich, *Scalp Dance: Indian Warfare on the High Plains, 1865-1879* (Mechanicsburg, PA: Stackpole Books, 1997), 43.

happen; we are just too afraid to admit that they do. For this reason, your community may have to orchestrate red team analyzes with the aid of outside professionals

To begin organizing more effective red team training simulations, authors Sloan and Bunker offer several basic principles:[31]

- *Simulations are not simple gaming or theoretical exercises.* They involve real world scenarios and take place at actual sites employing warm-blooded individuals in active positions rather than mere computer representations or white board maneuvers.

- *Participants do not engage within role-playing.* Red team exercises are not set on a stage with actors; they involve adversaries who live, breathe, and function as if a bona fide terrorists, active shooters, and disgruntled co-workers (stopping *just* short of actual killing).

- *Exercises must employ unscripted processes.* If your team knows what to *expect*, it should never fail. Despite that some terrorist organizations employ the same methods and targets for each of their attacks, *your* adversary may not simply resemble "some terrorists". Your red team exercise should literally catch you off your toes.

- *Avoid the exclusivity of too complex simulations.* Face it, your particular

---

[31] Sloan and Bunker, *Red Teams*, 16-31.

community will not be able to withstand a 9/11 or Mumbai, India style attack. Why, then, waste precious resources and time training for something that you will *not* be able to endure? Your simulations should involve a great deal of common sense, even if your "adversaries" do not; for to train for the patently unlikely merely diverts from the probable.

- *Simulations should not be micromanaged or "politically correct".* Your probable aggressors – whether organized terrorist, disenfranchised "lone wolf", or simple criminal – do not care about public sentiments or ethics. They represent inherently evil persons and will not avoid any activity to harm you. Accordingly, your red team operations must operate *as if* your adversaries and *not* as your co-workers pretending to be "bad". In other words, your red team unit or contractor should be realistic enough to keep you from sleeping at night.

- *Simulations should avoid 'worst case' focus.* For the duration of your community security and defense team's existence, the worst crisis that you *might* confront represents a drunken pedestrian. *Perhaps.* The truth is, you just never now. Therefore, your red team exercises must run the gamut of predictable and perceivable scenarios to ensure that your security team may be able to handle whatever it confronts – even if rather mundane.

- *Red team operations should offer anticipatory simulations as well.* If you have an intelligence unit, then it needs utilization. Too many simulations rest upon *reaction* to terrorist and criminal events. To keep your community's personnel on its toes, then attempt to determine what your red team unit will target *beforehand*. That is, red team your red team.

- *After-action debriefing.* Your people will not learn much if your organization does not effectively evaluate and honestly comment on your response to whatever the red team unit threw at you. You must consider what you did correctly, incorrectly, and not at all.

- *Involve your community within all simulations.* Anything that your particular facility or institution is likely to encounter will involve your broader community to a degree. Even a comparatively isolated event such as an active shooter will generate widespread media coverage, involve your state's leadership, and, perhaps, taint that community for a great many years. Therefore, you should always involve a portion of your community within simulations to aid with potential recuperative responses.

- *Simulations are not checklist functions.* Unlike preparing an airplane for flight, red team operations exist to challenge your cognitive processes and the response of your security teams, both of which involve *métis*. They are not to ensure that you perform actions as ordained by legislative protocol (as would be the case with *techne* doctrine).

With these red team principles in mind, we can now consider what "principles" terrorist organizations often follow.

At this point, perhaps, it might appear slightly pretentious to suggest that terrorists and other criminal organizations must follow any form of established principles for committing indiscriminate mayhem. As already discussed, narcotics trafficking organizations (as with jihadist terrorists) engage within brainstorming sessions to foster competitive adaptation. Such relaxed atmospheres do not hint at formulation of any type of principle or doctrine.

We can, however, attribute to *some* illicit organizations, terrorists included, principles similar to military special operations. Specifically, we can discuss six principles of that particular field developed by William H. McRaven. McRaven's principles include:[32]

1. *Simplicity.* As highly innovation functions, special operations remain simplistic at heart. The use of box cutters to hijack airliners as suicide aircraft or the detonation of bombs within crowded public facilities remain pure actions even if their broader programs remain complex.

2. *Security.* Disclosure can remain deadly for any organization, particularly ones engaged within illicit activities. Neither the 9/11 attacks nor homicide bombings would have succeeded if the participant's actions were

---

[32] William H. McRaven, *SPEC OPS: Case Studies in Special Operations Warfare: Theory and Practice* (New York: Ballantine Books/Presidio Press, 1996), 8-23.

flushed out. Because of this, many criminal or terrorist organizations retain tighter security measures than military organizations cursed with legislative oversight can.

3. *Repetition.* Success never rests upon the shoulders of chance, for training is not likely to be cemented into an individual's mind without adequate rehearsal. Perhaps more so than military special operations, terrorists possess limited resources and must therefore ensure that procedures and missions are ingrained within member's minds in order to affect expected results.

4. *Surprise.* Present hand in hand with security, surprise founds the hallmark of terrorist activities. To place public authority on the ropes and instill panic amongst the population, terrorists' activities are almost exclusively *surprise-centric* missions. Homicide bombings, for instance, recreate on a local level what the 9/11 attacks did for global civilization as a whole: they *surprise* the community with the introduction of the heretofore inconceivable.

5. *Speed.* Attrition-style wars, such as traditional guerrilla campaigns, are necessarily degrading to all parties concerned. The victor remains the side that can weather the greatest losses and this, almost exclusively, entails the party with more nation-state resources available to thrust into the conflict. Terrorist attacks, whether

human-launched or from passive device, represent swift strikes to devastate populations through induced shock.

6. *Purpose.* The purpose of terror may appear sacrilegious to many, but every terrorist incident in history held some measure of strategic value for the progenitors. A bombing may, for instance, punish an unsympathetic population or serve as retaliation against a foreign military incursion.

These six principles further shore the concept of *relative superiority*: "...a condition that exists when an attacking force, generally smaller, gains a decisive advantage over a larger or well-defended enemy."[33]

To succeed against your community, therefore, criminal organizations and individuals gain relative superiority *before* you can react in force or gain support from other agencies. Using the case of an active shooter, he or she bears a relatively short tangent towards superiority, one measured in minutes before his or her advantage tapers off due to police or internal response (See Figure 18).

A homicide bomber, naturally, bears a starker line of superiority as his or her job remains to sneak into an unsuspecting community and blow themselves apart. Because of this, their relative superiority ends with the destruction of her or her life – unless intelligence or eyewitnesses penetrate his or her secrecy.

Coordinated operations, such as the Mumbai India attacks of November 2008, suggest a broader line of gaining relative superiority that peaks at the moment of the first shootings to then taper off slowly as local authorities respond and citizens bunker down.

With these basic principles in mind, your community response plan (and red team training) can visualize some "method to the madness" of terrorist attacks. They do not represent spontaneous actions of a disgruntled employee nor an "insane" individual. During the Vietnam conflict, for example, both the North Vietnamese Army and the Vietcong "blatantly used atrocity as a policy and [were] triumphant because of it."[34] One could not conclude that an entire nation was "insane" nor where their widespread assassinations of South Vietnamese officials "spontaneous" in nature.

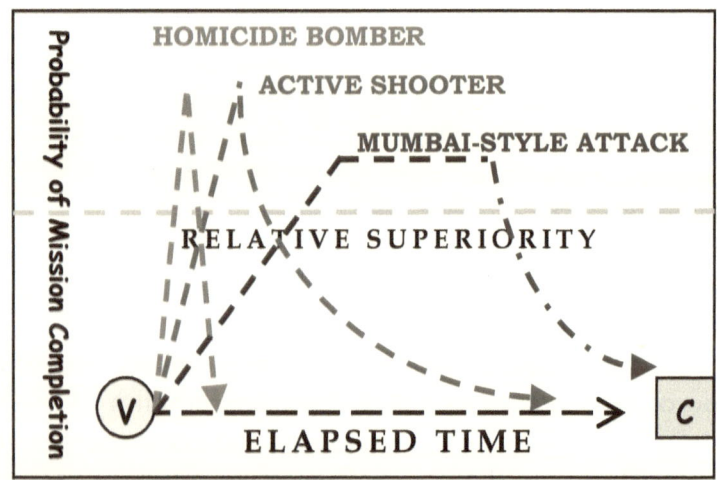

Figure 18. McRaven Concept of Relative Superiority.
Key: Point of Vulnerability (V), Mission Completion (C).

Red team functions must take both inherent brutality and legitimate, rational planning into mind

---

[33] Ibid., 4.
[34] Dave Grossman, *On Killing: The Psychological Cost of Learning to Kill in War and Society* (New York: Back Bay Books, 2009), 209-210.

when orchestrating "attacks" for your security and defense personnel to confront. For the United States, while concerns remain high regarding Islamic jihadists, particular involving threats from ISIS, the nation faces more indiscriminate threats from its southern neighbors. In this context, we need only to address two groups from present and recent history.

La Familia Michoacana. The now-defunct *La Familia* drug tracking group represented a Middle Eastern-esque fusion of intense religious beliefs – in this particular case, fantastical views of Biblical history – and abject brutality to instill fear and corral members into behaving. One of *La Familia's* notorious instances of sending a "big message" was to hack off the heads of five individuals from a local mechanic's shop with butcher knives and then throw the severed heads onto a crowded dance floor declaring their "divine justice" to kill anyone that interfered with their operations.[35]

Los Zetas. Another Mexican drug organization that employs the beheadings of police officers as its version of divine justice, known as "'the most technically advanced, sophisticated, and violent' private army in Mexico" hails from former Mexico army special forces personnel trained in "rapid deployment, aerial assaults, marksmanship, ambushes, intelligence collection, counter-surveillance techniques, prisoner rescues, sophisticated communications, and the art of *intimidation* [emphasis added]".[36] This group remains

---

[35] George W. Grayson, *La Familia Drug Cartel: Implications for U.S.-Mexican Security* (Carlisle, PA: Strategic Studies Institute, December 2010), 1.

[36] Hal Brands, *Mexico's Narco-Insurgency and U.S. Counterdrug Policy* (Carlisle, PA: Strategic Studies Institute, May 2009), 8.

currently active.

If we only take these two particular groups, we understand that ISIS-style beheadings are neither unusual nor distant. Narco-traffickers have been beheading people for decades and reside just across America's southern border (though present reports suggest that they have deeply invaded the United States). Furthermore, in the case of *Los Zetas*, this massive "private army" bears equipment and expertise that ISIS, al-Qaeda, and other jihadist groups could only dream of – leading to suspected cooperation between the divergent groups. That ISIS is reportedly active in all fifty U.S. states, as per the Federal Bureau of Investigation (FBI), serves to authenticate this as, undoubtedly, *Los Zetas* flooded into the United States long ago (see Figure 19).

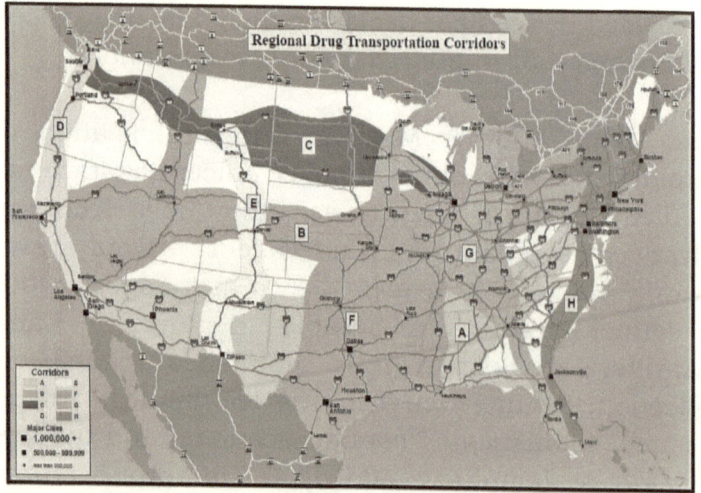

Figure 19. Drug Trafficking Corridors within the United States. Source: U.S. Department of Justice (http://www.justice.gov/archive/ndic/pubs38/38661/images/figure3.jpg)

Even if your community represents a renowned university, it remains unlikely that your staff bears the experience and capabilities to plan for *Los Zetas*-style raids on your campus. Therefore, you *must* differ to professionals that can mimic such organizations through red team operations. Simply having internal staff or, perhaps, local police officers masquerading in the role merely represents playing with fire – and human lives. Even a casual observation of Figure 19 shows that the vast majority of colleges and universities within the United States exist within these drug trafficking corridors.

Undoubtedly, your university – or high school or hospital – has already suffered from the influences of *Los Zetas* and, quite probably, ISIS as well. Red team utilization will permit concerned administrations an ability to detect – as well as predict – narcotics sales within your environment. This intelligence could be used to build profiles on potential threats from active shooters on through terroristic attacks.[37]

During the Cold War – and even today, albeit on a different format – the U.S. Air Force conducted 'Red Flag' operations to train new pilots over the Nevada deserts. The "enemy" pilots flew older American jets that resembled Soviet designs, spoke exclusively Russian, and lived in barracks that bore Russian newspapers, Soviet posters, and filtered Russian music. These American pilots were, for all intents and purposes, "Red Soviet" adversaries that kept "kill ratios" of the dirty rotten capitalists that they "shot down" out of the sky.

For their role, the Soviet Union took the concept

---

[37] Admittedly, "profiling" implies a racist or bigoted concept in modern society, but *your* function remains to protect human lives – *not* keep from offending groups. Living people can – and will – recover.

a bit further, building entire towns and villages that resembled in the smallest of details cities and towns within the United States. Their "residents" listened to rock-and-roll music, attended church on Sundays, and many even enjoyed "hotdogs, apple pies and Chevrolets..."

This Soviet concept went further than merely training pilots in how to fight 'unfriendlies', they conditioned their saboteurs in how to infiltrate American communities. They could, in effect, take any one of their agents and drop them within the heart of Main Street, U.S.A. and American citizens would never know that the new resident within their ranks was a Soviet mole awaiting word to contaminate water supplies, indoctrinate students in school, or even seeking public office.

This represents the mentality behind red team personnel – they may be Americans, for instance, deeply devoted to his or her country. As patriotic as you are, perhaps even more so. Yet, his or her job is to *function* as an Islamic jihadist or a South American drug trafficker. They speak, not English, but Arabic or Spanish. They see vulnerabilities within every aspect of society and are ready to exploit that weakness to "kill" as many people as they can. And, folks, they do not lose a minute of sleep over it. Neither will you if your community effectively employs his or her talents to combat prior to the *real thing* arriving.

13. HARDENING THE SCHOOL

NOT quite as bad as churches, for instance, schools, colleges, and universities represent the most difficult institutions to secure against aggression. Part of this problem rests with their function – the education and training of a nation's youth. That is, probably ninety-percent (90%) of those occupying the premises are there because he or she does not hold enough experience to survive in the outside world. They remain little more than lumps of clay waiting to move around, not quite old enough to possess the vast numbers of others' "fingerprints" upon their soul that define maturity.

The other part of the reason that educational institutions remain lax in security is that school administrations bear little knowledge in 'real world' environments. Most university professors, for example, remain in tenure while his or her course doctrine is fashioned many years in advance in order to accommodate accreditation standards. Educational institutions simply cannot adjust fast enough to deal with innovative threats or global revolutions. Yet, there is a third, less publicized though no less important reason that schools and colleges remain difficult to secure. *Attitude.*

As pillars of their respective communities,

schools simply do not feel threatened enough to take protective measures. After all, *who* wants to disrupt the lives of a nation's most innocent persons? *What* motivation could an individual or group possess that would force them to actually target a population of the most innocent of all?

For those that could not remember – or simply did not know about – the May 18, 1927 massacre in Bath, Michigan, Eric Harris and Dylan Klebold answered the question with their diabolical attack at Columbine High School in Littleton, Colorado on April 20, 1999. They killed twelve students and one teacher. Despite that their horrendous assault resulted in only about *one-quarter* the casualties of the Kehoe massacre in Bath, this seminal incident politicized the debate over school violence for the next several decades. It represented the defining moment in the realization that not only were schools targeted for simply being schools, but that such institutions were amongst the least prepared to deal with major catastrophes.

Yet, the lesson remained relatively benign – as is often the case, American introduction to crisis betrayed an inner selfishness that suggested that the United States remained the *only* nation on earth where tragedy should shock the world. The thirteen deaths at Columbine, for instance, broke the bounds of what America considered newsworthy.

To illustrate the point, the Beslan school siege began on September 1, 2004 when Chechen terrorists took 1,200 people hostage with guns and explosive devices, and they *were not afraid to kill the innocent to prove their intentions*. When the debris ultimately settled, 186 children, 158 adults, 4 emergency workers, and 11 Special Forces soldiers were dead with another 700 hostages and 19 soldiers wounded.[38]

In terms of student deaths alone, the Beslan tragedy equated with almost five Bath and sixteen Columbine massacres, attesting to the notion that the world remains far deadlier than Americans, or Westerners, care to admit. None of the notable American school shootings, for instance, involved the deaths of police officers or emergency workers. Neither were any of the school shootings multi-day sieges. Nor were any of the attackers trained and discipline paramilitary organizations.

Thus, the first step within school security rests with confronting reality. Even the April 16, 2007 shooting at Virginia Polytechnic Institute and State University ("Virginia Tech"), carried out by a lone gunman in two distinct attacks, paled in comparison to either the Bath or Beslan massacres. This more recent atrocity killed 32 and wounded another 12 individuals. The most recent shooting, in relation to this writing, the October 1, 2015 shooting at Umpqua Community College near Roseburg, Oregon killed nine persons while injuring another nine.

Statistically, these horrendous events remain little more unsettling than aviation disasters. Nevertheless, their apparent "frequency" – as suggested by media and political hype – suggests that society is coming unglued at the seams. Here, reality mandates that school administrators and staff reflect upon the numbers.

In 2015, there are an estimated 50.1 million students enrolled within elementary and secondary

---

[38] Michael J. McMains and Wayman C. Mullins, *Crisis Negotiations: Managing Critical Incidents and Hostage Situations in Law Enforcement and Corrections, Fourth Edition* (New Providence, NJ: Anderson Publishing, 2010), 42.

schools within the United States.[39] The total enrollment within the nation's colleges and universities is about 20.6 million.[40] If we employ a baseline school year of 180 days for students of all elementary-to-collegiate educational institutions, we gain some perspective in gauging these atrocities.

For example, if we were to experience a Bath-style massacre *every day of the school year,* we would arrive at 38 x 180 = 6,840 children killed. This translates into 6,840/50,100,000 equals 0.00014 or *0.014%* of the total student population. Similarly, if we experienced a Virginia Tech-style massacre *every day of the school year,* we would arrive at 32 x 180 = 5,760 persons killed. This translates into 5,760/20,600,000 equals approximately 0.00030 or *0.03%* of the nation's post-secondary population.

Again, for perspective, we can utilize other figures. For instance, 1,825 college students succumb each year from unintentional alcohol-related deaths.[41] Similarly, 2,163 licensed teenagers die each year from automobile-related accidents.[42] The above figures prove that both school shootings and related massacres are not as frequent as the media or politicians would suggest. In fact, if we were to multiply the singularity of Bath, Michigan *one hundred and eighty times,* we would only approximate 6840/3988 = 1.72 times the number of students killed by alcohol and teenaged driving.

Backed by these numbers, we can dismiss the

[39]http://nces.ed.gov/fastfacts/display.asp?id=372. Accessed October 2015.

[40] http://nces.ed.gov/fastfacts/display.asp?id=98. Accessed October 2015.
[41]http://www.niaaa.nih.gov/alcohol-health/special-populations-co-occurring-disorders/college-drinking. Accessed October 2015.
[42]http://www.cdc.gov/motorvehiclesafety/teen_drivers/teendrivers_factsheet.html. Accessed October 2015.

hysteria involving school and university shootings within the United States and the world. They do *not* mean that your school or university should ignore the potentiality for active shooter situations. Rather, you must continue to plan for the expected and what others experience, you *may* witness. At a minimum, these numbers suggest that the relative rarity of school shootings and bombings suggest that they appear quite random, without an opportunity for human terrain mapping – the process by which social data is projected upon territory – to develop probability targets.

When any information remains at a premium, the best solution is to keep such activities in the back of your mind whenever dealing with perceived threats. That gunmen attack schools does not mean that *your particular* school is threatened with an attack. Rather, that your field is exposed to a comparable evil much as how U.S. post offices witnessed forty individuals shot by co-workers during the period 1986-1997, giving rise to the slang "going postal" in America. Today, such shootings have disappeared, though work-related violence remains a key security consideration.

For your school or university, you must develop a threat response diagram as shown in Figure 20. This tool will aid you in determining your own community's focus upon security and defense. Once this response analysis is completed, you will be able to consider the suggestions outlined within this chapter. The higher you suffer the threat, the more time and resources you must devote to that particular response (knowing that you must prepare for *all* contingencies nonetheless).

You will be able to reduce the hysterics involved with reaction – and publicity – as well as provide damage control rebuttals following crises. Such tools provide a foundation upon which to corral guesswork, hyperbole, and, perhaps, opportunistic security contractors. Every function or thought that you undertake must be subject to your conscience and procedural plan – otherwise you will suffer to emotions.

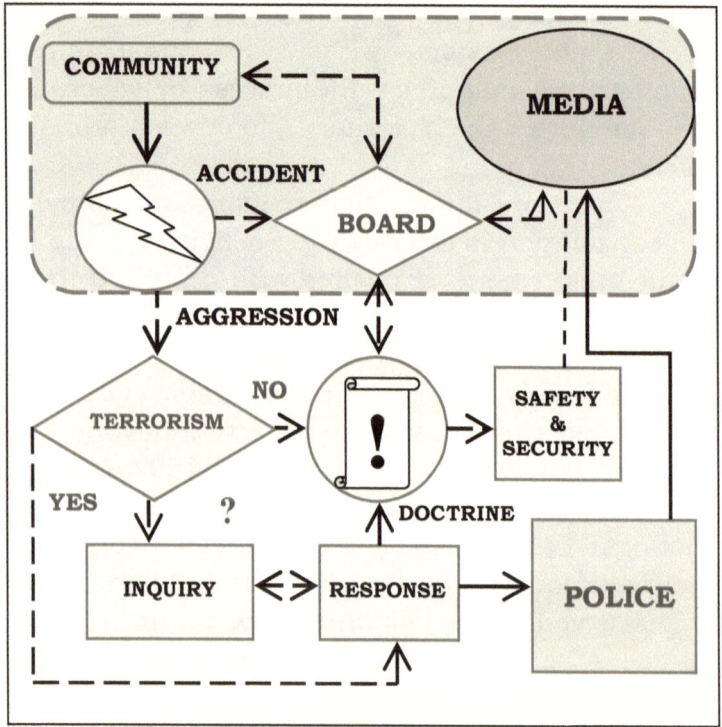

Figure 20. Sample Threat Response Chart.

Coinciding with threat response planning is, of course, categorization of threat probabilities. One cannot realistically develop one without the other or focus primarily upon one side of the issue. You must know how you would respond to certain threats even if you may not know what those threats entail. In other words, you require both perception and consideration.

	Large University	Local College	Secondary School	Elementary School
Active Shooter	7	6	4	3
Suicide Bomber	5	4	2	2
Domestic Violence	8	6	4	3
Civil Unrest	8	6	2	2
Terrorist Attack	4	4	3	2
Severe Weather	9	9	8	8
Fire	6	6	5	4
Power Outage	2	2	2	2
Missing Person(s)	4	3	3	2
VIP Visit	8	7	7	2

Figure 21. Threat probability matrix for educational institutions. Higher numbers represent greater risks.

Figure 21 represents a threat probability matrix that will aid community planners in determining the potential for various emergencies affecting your security. Such a chart rests as a guide since no two schools or universities remain the same. For instance, a prestigious secondary school (e.g., military, parochial, etc.) may actually witness more occurrences of VIP visits than many larger colleges. Similarly, older schools will suffer greater occurrences of fire and power outages than newer facilities.

Once you determine the probabilities for your

particular school or university, you must then develop procedural doctrine for dealing with those specific threats. Such procedural doctrine does not represent what your staff *will* do; rather it lays the foundational procedures that your personnel should undertake in an "ideal" situation while allowing for maximum flexibility.

Some procedures to consider should include the following and build upon material contained within previous chapters:

Active Shooters: Any active shooter incident represents one of the most terrifying scenarios any citizen could face. In the school setting with a captive, youthful population, the situation becomes even more troubling. To emerge successfully from this crisis, you must possess procedural policies regarding the following.

- ✓ *Fight or flee.* To retain advantage over aggressors, you must undertake actions that he or she is less likely to expect. Since the most common reaction may be to barricade in place without resistance, you must consider evacuation as rapidly and as safely as possible since, again, moving persons remain harder to target. The second option – rendering lethal resistance – represents the most dangerous and, perhaps, unexpected response (but one that you may have no other recourse to consider).

- ✓ *Arming your staff.* If you choose to fight aggression, then you bear a multitude of considerations. First, *who* shall represent your defensive force? A professionally trained rapid reaction force? Teachers and professors? Any licensed adult citizen? Secondly, *what* type of firearms will you allow within your property? Smaller caliber handguns? Large-capacity carbines and rifles (primarily consisting of the much hated "assault weapons")? Whatever a person holding such a license prefers to carry? Next, what about ammunition? Will you restrict firearms to carrying frangible rounds only (and thereby reducing firearm selection) for safety? Will you prefer hollow-point ammunition to offer the best chance of stopping the aggressor?

✓ *Community warning system.* When an active shooter situation occurs, *how* will you warn your community to the danger? In a small school, there may be no need to sound such a warning, but with a large college campus, the word must be distinctively transmitted to *all* individuals on the premises. Does this entail broad cellular telephone text messages? What if students or visitors do not possess telephones or have it turned off? Do you then enact a tornado-like warning klaxon that may be heard over a great distance? If so, how will your population respond? Have you trained them sufficiently enough to act accordingly?

✓ *Incident central command.* Do you possess a central command that will employ video cameras and security communications to direct the flow of fleeing individuals? Or have you always deferred to the law enforcement community? Any active aggression means that the "police option" has already failed; you must consider what to do when *you* represent your community's last line of defense. This requires some measure of a "take command" unit that, at a minimum, directs operations until the local police arrive. In any active shooter situation, *speed* counts and you may not have the fifteen to forty-minutes to wait for police response.

Suicide bombers. With such groups as ISIS functioning within every conceivable location, you may witness a suicide bombing attack before you suffer through an active shooter situation. If this assessment remains valid, then you have less time to prepare for his or her arrival than with perhaps any other aggression.

- ✓ *Fighting is no longer an option.* Whereas a single (or even pair of) active shooter bears difficulty in targeting rapidly moving persons, a homicide bomber retains no such difficulty. Depending upon the explosive device used, individuals within your community may not possess sufficient time to vacate the lethal range of the bomb safely – especially since it undoubtedly carries shrapnel to increase its lethality. In this situation, you *must* render lethal force upon the aggressor.

- ✓ *How to prepare for "rendering the aggressor unable to inflict harm"?* Yours is a community of tens of thousands of students and faculty inhabiting hundreds of acres and dozens of towering buildings. A homicide bomber literally attacks a two-foot-wide section of that campus with a lethal range approximating 150 feet indoors and 1,850 feet outdoors.[43] *Whom* is your community going to possess within that location that can *stop* the aggressor before he or she detonates their device? How many such individuals are required to successfully cover your entire property or campus?

✓ *What about the aftermath?* Assuming that you cannot stop a suicide bomber due to the size of your particular community, *what* are your procedures for dealing with the aftermath? Will you have sufficient medical personnel available to treat the injured and prevent further deaths? Will your community be sufficiently trained to avoid contaminating forensic evidence? Does your facility bear enough room to stage ambulances and land helicopters? What are your procedures for such activities?

Terrorist attacks. Homicide bombers are not the *only* terrorists that may target your facility as the residents of Beslan learned in 2004. A legitimate invasion of weapons-toting terrorists on the magnitude of Beslan staggers the civilian imagination. If you were not confronted with a war during an active shooter or homicide-bombing incident, then there could be no other definition than when the time comes that several highly trained aggressors start feeding on your flock.

---

[43] James T. Thurman, *Practical Bomb Scene Investigation, Second Edition* (Boca Raton, FL: CRC/Taylor & Francis, 2011), 467.

✓ *Fleeing is the only option.* Let us face it; even public SWAT teams are ill equipped and poorly trained for dealing with combat veterans (which most organized terrorists are these days). At a minimum, they will be too far away and few in number to save your community from a siege. It remains *possible* that your security staff may orchestrate some measure of defense, but they will be unable to withstand a concerted attack for any length of time. For this reason alone, fleeing rests as your only option.

✓ *Safe egress routes are mandatory.* When dozens or hundreds of people begin fleeing in every direction under the sun, *how* will you direct them to the shortest route to safety? *What* training have you emplaced community-wide that will ensure his or her rapid egress under *varying* situations? How will you *warn* your campus or facility of the arrival of such numerous aggressors?

✓ *How will your community provide intelligence to the authorities?* If your school or university is overrun with terrorists, then it becomes a major international crisis (especially if you bear foreign students). How will you *retrieve* and *communicate* vital information to the appropriate authorities for use in negotiations and, perhaps, rescue? Are you *prepared* to sacrifice some staff in order to have them report such information through previously agreed upon and clandestine methods?

Other security-related events such as domestic violence disputes (irate spouse, etc.), civil unrest (rioting or rambunctious sports fans), and others can be handled through traditional campus/school security procedures worked out with local law enforcement. What must be considered, however, is whether any of these incidents involve larger threats, such as the use of the WTO protests in Seattle during 1999 by the Black Bloc anarchists to disrupt an entire metropolitan city.

The key for your community is to make efficient use of limited personnel, funds, and resources available to your security and defense operations. Traditionally, schools and universities have used "security" for such mundane tasks as checking identification badges and ensuring locked doors. While collectively following under the broad term of "security", these functions can be handled by *anyone* already on the institution's payroll. For instance, your janitorial staff may be able to verify locked doors as employing a night-shift janitorial crew will be more cost-effective than saddling professional security teams with entry-level "guards".

In combating – there remains no more appropriate word – aggression against your school or university, you *must* employ *force-multiplication*[44] against the threat. Diverting security personnel or trained individuals towards commonsense duties represents just such a distraction. So, too, remains the traditional approach of placing retired or off-duty

---

[44] Briefly, a "force multiplier" remains anything that increases the effectiveness of an individual or group of individuals (such as a military unit) where no such increase in efficiency would be permitted without that particular tactic or technology.

police officers (as is the rule for many states) into positions of providing security for institutions and businesses. This process violates the distinctive roles each discipline plays (see Figure 22).

Figure 22. How police agencies, security organizations, and militaries compare.

As you will note, security organizations are not limited in procedure or in jurisdiction as are police departments, but they do not hold the lethality and ability to deploy so broadly as with militaries. Nevertheless, security organizations bridge the gap between municipal contract and military oath. That is, for *true* security professionals, the duty to "prevent and deter" becomes a *covenant* – a solemn pledge to protect without abandon.

If your community employs "guards" to check ID badges and locked doors or "off duty" police officers to provide protection, then it is simply diluting the concept of force-multiplication. This is accomplished by placing individuals into position that, perhaps, hold no allegiance to the duty for which he or she is hired. The casual guard may simply be working to pay for school or to earn additional money until something better comes along. An off-duty police officer is *certainly* padding his or her income. Both simply view the function as an addendum to his or her other interests.

If this remains the case, then it is far better to *add* such responsibilities to others already on your community's payroll. Perhaps, even, increase the wage of a janitor that checks locked doors or of a receptionist who inspects identification badges. Both options will save your institution money over hiring a "dedicated" guard for either function. The key to remember is that security remains *everyone's* function during the 21st century and you must employ all personnel within your security doctrine, even if in a minor role.

Most individuals remain quite able to *prevent*, through either locking doors or monitoring suspicious visitors. These functions represent relatively *passive* duties that require very little training or forethought. In fact, most people do these activities freely out of personal fear; you just need to convince them to transfer this subconscious activity to work.

Deterrence, however, may require *active* response on the part of your security personnel. Alarm systems and dogs may "deter", but at some point, a criminal will simply bypass the alarms or render dogs impotent (through one of several methods). In this case, more substantive measures of deterrence will be called upon – including the use of lethal force. If this becomes the case, then only a *professional* security operation will be able to deal with the aftermath.

Few – and, yes, there are individuals that will

challenge *any* action – will reel in horror over security personnel shooting and killing someone about to denote a nuclear device in the middle of a major city, particular his or her own. It could even be assumed that such security personnel would be correctly hailed as heroes.

That said, draw down the scenario to involve an abductor, a rapist, an active shooter or, even, a suicide bomber, and the critics will flow from the proverbial woodwork as if ants seeking to salivate over a new found pile of sugar. Crowds will clamor against "brutality" and civil rights attorneys will stumble over one another litigating in the millions of dollars. Here is where your community must scrutinize your chosen security team and much is learned from observing how the three disciplines outlined in Figure 22 will respond.

First, police departments remain municipal agencies and, therefore, internal review boards will convene to decipher both intent and outcome. One or more officers are likely to be placed on "administrative leave" to determine if anyone's civil rights were violated. This action, taken to placate members of the public, may even go as far as to initiate settlements to ensure that taxpayers do not erupt into riots. Lives may have been saved, but as with doting parents, politicians are not interested in justice – they want peace and quiet.

If a military force undertook the action – presumably overseas, as American forces are unable to operate within the United States itself – then certainly there would be a Congressional oversight committee to achieve much the same results as the internal review board does for police shootings. In this case, massively televised hearings would, eventually, lead to padded legislation that undoubtedly only passes because the Senate and House add numerous attachments bearing little to do with the killing of a gunman or homicide bomber.

For their role, professional security companies offer several distinct advantages over either the police or the military. First, they represent *private* operations that remain staffed with *private citizens* that represent, in context, taxpayers as well. Well-managed security companies further uphold ethical standards that exceed, in some cases, both law enforcement and military entities. This is because security companies can be as discriminating – or as lax – as possible.

Second, professional security companies operate as "security warriors"; that is, they view the whole concept of defense as a *lifestyle* and holistic discipline. This means that they take *protection* and defense to a level of commitment unattainable by police departments. These "defenders of innocent human lives" will not acquiesce to legislation or litigation – if they have to employ lethal force to save these lives.

Politicians, by nature, are often referred to as "cowards". It could be argued, however, that the vast majority of human beings, particularly citizens of Western nations, remain cowardly in life. He or she simply wants to enjoy the conveniences of modern civilization without anything disrupting the status quo. What they do *not* want is to experience litigation or negative publicity. This is why municipalities often defer to settlement even if their police officers acted correctly.

Security professionals understand how to turn the advantage in favor of their clients. They know how to exert psychological warfare to place critics on the defensive. This is accomplished through publicity campaigns, social media programs, and counter-litigation. *Anything* that disrupts the tranquility of bureaucrats. Unfortunately, mere "guards" will not be able to protect your community within a similar manner.

Most institutions gamble on their security operations, preferring to spend as little as possible on protection and deterrence. When something major happens, they immediately shift to insurance and/or taxpayer-funded recovery programs. Neither needs to be the case, however, because effective security remains both low-cost and proactive. It will protect you before, during, and after incidents occur. To protect your school or university you must become more *militant* if not military in nature.

14. HARDENING HEALTHCARE

FOR Western nations, the vulnerability of hospitals and other healthcare facilities rests rarely discussed, primarily because such places of "healing" remain protected through international standards of respect and recognition. We have all seen war movies where the ubiquitous ambulance emblazoned with a big, red cross on its side races into the front to save a wounded patriot of the cause.

Unfortunately, during the 21st century that symbol of medical personnel has morphed into a target for criminal and terrorist groups upon which to fix his or her sights. More importantly, in the regions where most conflicts occur, any symbol relating to Christianity is both discouraged *and* an affront to local sensibilities. The Red Cross is as strange to them as the Red Crescent remains to us, though they essentially represent the same organization.

Nevertheless, the key consideration remains that hospitals, healthcare clinics, and related facilities are targeted today by groups that care less about Western institutions. As an example, Osama bin Laden's al-Qaeda functions according to his *fatwa*:

"The ruling to kill the Americans and their allies – civilians and military – is an individual duty for every Muslim who can do it in any country in which it is possible to do it.... every Muslim who believes in God and wishes to be rewarded to comply with God's order to kill the Americans and plunder their money wherever and whenever they find it."

There remain no limitations to this doctrine to kill *all* Americans – civilians and military – and plunder their money.

Other Islamic groups such as ISIS have made a point to attack those institutions whose targeting will unnerve a majority of the population. These efforts are essentially psychological operations more than military ones, for their role remains to shock and intimidate civilians into submission. In fact, many of these groups intentionally place ammunition and weapons into hospitals in order to induce U.S. or Western airstrikes on these facilities, thereby creating collateral damage involving innocent men, women, and children.

Nevertheless, violence against hospitals is neither exclusively modern nor Islamic in origin. There has been violence perpetrated against medical facilities for as long as there have been individuals who exercised his or her grievances through aggression. They care little about where or under what circumstances their actions take place. Rather, they merely undertake violence in areas easily accessible to their mentality and time. An individual, therefore, remains as likely to lose control within a convenience store as he or she is likely to erupt within a hospital. That said, a patient angry with a doctor or an-ex spouse confronting a nurse on the job is more likely to involve hospitals than those convenience stores.

Accordingly, the first step in securing

healthcare facilities – contrasting, somewhat, with educational institutions – is to recognize that they represent legitimate targets for *anyone* with a grudge or hatred towards the institution, its staff, or its patients. They no longer represent "no go" zones for criminals and terrorists under some form of international diplomatic treaty. Healthcare facilities, in the 21st century, are legitimate targets in the minds of those who hate any particular group.

Acknowledging this, we can begin threat assessments for your particular facility:

	Regional Hospital	Medical Clinic	Therapeutic Center	Specialty Clinic
Active Shooter	7	6	6	6
Suicide Bomber	5	4	4	4
Domestic Violence	8	6	7	7
Civil Unrest	8	6	2	2
Terrorist Attack	4	4	3	2
Severe Weather	7	7	8	8
Fire	6	6	5	4
Power Outage	2	2	3	3
Missing Person(s)	6	3	5	2
VIP Visit	8	7	7	8

Figure 23. Threat probability matrix for healthcare facilities. Therapeutic centers include substance abuse clinics, etc. Specialty clinics include sports rehabilitation clinics, abortion clinics, etc.

More so than educational institutions, perhaps, healthcare facilities cover a wide range of divergent and interconnected institutions, each bearing a unique threat environment. For instance, large regional hospitals may contain smaller units, substance abuse and psychiatric clinics, as well as a host of rehabilitative centers for sports and occupational therapy. As such, these facilities score high in all assessment categories with the exception of experiencing power outages – as small cities in and of themselves, major hospitals retain better backup systems than smaller offices.

Smaller, more specialized clinics present significant probabilities for VIP visitations and, in the case of substance abuse centers, missing persons, when compared with similar-sized educational institutions. This is due to the number of professional athletes and entertainers that exemplify visitors to such facilities. Such patients further level the potential occurrence for active shooters and domestic violence due to, amongst other concerns, inherent wealth and fame and the presence of unstable individuals.

Domestic violence issues, which include irate spouses, disgruntled patients, etc. for the purposes of this book, also feature prominently due to the health and concerns of people frequenting these establishments. Whereas educational institutions concentrate youths into vulnerable locations, healthcare facilities place vulnerable individuals into concentrated groups that remain likely to draw hateful or aggressive individuals.

More importantly, however, medical facilities also accumulate valuable pharmaceuticals, instrumentation, and support systems (gases, chemicals, hazardous materials, etc.) into well-defined and accessible locations. Criminals, for instance, seeking narcotics or radioactive materials target hospitals and medical research facilities at a higher rate than educational institutions.

Because of their diversity, healthcare facilities place three distinct burdens upon security personnel:

1. Healthcare facilities remain populated with individuals under severe distress. Nearly every visitor remains either a patient or someone escorting a patient. During even relatively minor disturbances, they will not act in the same manner as they would if not burdened with illness or caretaking.

2. Patients and other visitors to healthcare facilities are not likely to represent "routine" guests – as would be the case with students at a university – and therefore they are quite unfamiliar with the layout of the facility particularly that involving the location of emergency exists, stairwells, fire extinguishers, and first-aid stations. In any crisis, they may simply freeze or panic.

3. Healthcare institutions bear more critical infrastructure than, say, educational facilities. The latter amounts to little more than traditional offices punctuated with high-tech laboratories, classrooms, etc. In contrast, hospitals, for their role, retain life-saving or life-support equipment within virtually every space outside patient waiting rooms. During active shooting incidents, great care must be made not to damage or destroy this equipment.

Figure 24 illustrates some of these concerns.

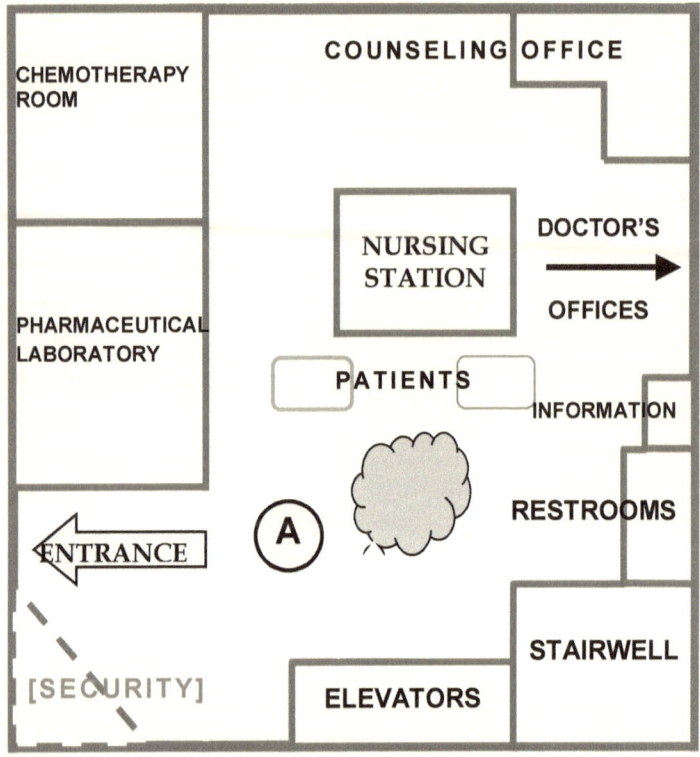

Figure 24. Sample hospital environment. Key: (A) Active shooter/Aggressor

We see some of the critical issues involved with hospital security through examining the presence of an active shooter or other aggressor (denoted by A). If the security response team arrives by way of elevator or stairwell, they immediately confront a (potentially) armed assailant a mere few feet away. If they draw to shoot, then their bullets may travel pass the aggressor and enter the pharmaceutical laboratory or chemotherapy treatment room, potentially fatally injuring staff or patients that, under these circumstances, may be bound to chairs and beds through medical tubes.

On the other hand, if the security team arrives from outside the floor through the building entrance, then their line of fire involves waiting patients, the nursing station, persons in the counseling rooms, and anyone near the entrance to the physician's examination rooms. Either case involves an aggressor with freedom to move versus a severally restricted security team.

In this case, with limited options, it remains best to place a security post against the exterior wall adjacent to the entrance door (refer to Figure 3 as well). This vantage point allows security personnel to detect threats as they emerge from any of the three entrances to the floor. For aggressors entering the building from the outside, security would have essentially appeared from *behind* the aggressor, granting tactical advantage to the protective services team. In each case, should the security team have to fire upon the aggressor, their line of sight, at worst, places the building's non-inhabited rooms (stairwell, etc.) behind the aggressor.

While this illustration remains exceedingly simple, the reader should observe basic security principles inherent within healthcare facilities. These site-specific conditions ensure that hospital and healthcare defense will tax both the personnel and resources of your community. Perhaps more so than any other "community" outlined within this book, healthcare institutions provide a complex fusion of social, industrial, educational, and service-related activities within a highly populated environment.

This requires protective services personnel to be uniquely qualified within human thought perception, federal and indigenous laws, social interaction, and tactical deployment – attributes shared by other security fields but not to the same, universal degree.

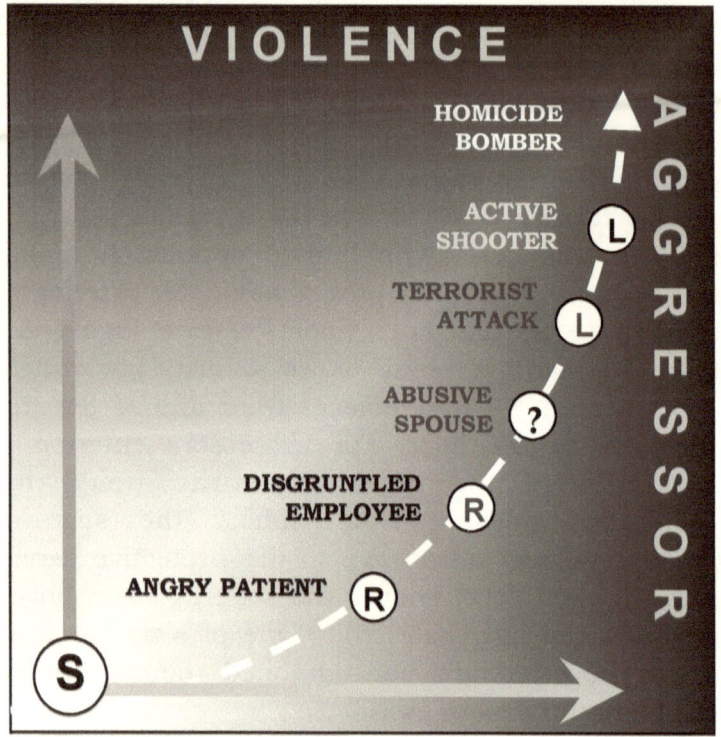

Figure 25. Violence-Aggression Proximity Chart. As security personnel confront ever-increasing aggression, he or she must progress from merely restraining belligerent persons to employing lethal force.

Not all situations will involve force to subdue belligerent individuals. For example, the confrontation of a patient distraught over waiting to see a physician in the emergency room does not require a maximum use of force. Similarly, a disgruntled employee may simply be angry over a shortage in his or her paycheck or, possibly, a poor performance evaluation. In this particular situation, restraint may not even be required if security personnel can persuade them to head home to cool off.

However, an abusive spouse represents someone that has *already exhibited violent behavior* and, as such, security may not be aware of his or her intent. Such an individual may be a wife who merely threatened to "bash in the head" of a husband whom she saw smiling at another woman or an ex-husband with an active restraining order filed against him. Such 'borderline' scenarios mean that security personnel must retain active files on all violent staff and their families and proceed with extreme caution.

It is when the progression of threat turns to terrorists, active shooters, and homicide bombers that lethal force becomes expected. The latter two scenarios, due to their singular urgency, rest just above terrorist attacks (i.e., group initiated) on the scale of violence as a means of ending aggression (see Figure 25). With a more significant number of the residing population – i.e., patients – as opposed to students or parishioners – remaining relatively immobile, the security staff within a hospital or other major healthcare facility must remain ready to takedown aggressors as quickly as possible.

This is *not* to imply that healthcare security professionals must be trigger-happy mercenaries ready to do battle at the earliest opportunity. On the contrary, healthcare security personnel must be responsible, tolerant, and *highly trained* individuals that can tell the difference between aggression and anger, between violence and terrorism, and between *professionals* and pirates.[45]

It remains for this reason, primarily, that medical communities cannot differ to public involvement as much as, say, within the educational community. While it has been known, for instance, that some emergency room personnel, including attending physicians, have armed him or herself within the more dangerous areas of the country, their primary function is to serve injured and ill patients. They simply do not possess the time to deal with aggressive individuals – ordinarily.

There remain several scenarios where healthcare institutions *must* rely upon armed staff and/or visitors:

1. An incident occurs where an active shooter or a suicide bomber materializes within an unexpected location and hospital staff remains the only personnel within response range. As shown within Figure 25, active shooters and suicide bombers require *immediate* action as any delay will lead to deaths.

2. An external incident occurs where incapacitation of a vehicular driver is required to prevent the automobile or truck (ostensibly suspected as a vehicular-borne improvised explosive device, or VBIED) from crashing into a vulnerable portion of the medical facility not under direct observation of any security forces.

---

[45] "Pirate" is a term that author Dick Couch employs to describe those few individuals that sour the reputation of an otherwise professional unit and lead decent persons astray. See Dick Couch, *A Tactical Ethic: Moral Conduct in the Insurgent Battlespace* (Annapolis, MD: Naval Institute Press, 2010), 5-6.

3. The hospital or clinic remains too small and, perhaps, too remotely located to staff a full-time security team (paid or otherwise).

4. Local municipal authorities prevent the hospital staff from employing a security detail, in which case severe threat response relegates to citizens violating the law.

Any one of these incidents and, conceivably, a great many more conspire to place Western healthcare facilities in danger and the reliance for survival falls upon dedicated members of society.

Nevertheless, simply receiving ordination to install a security team – paid or volunteer – does not automatically convey any sense of security upon *any* institution, and medical facilities remain no exception to the rule. Before a team can be put into place, several concerns must be addressed exclusive to the healthcare industry. Questions answered that may not arise from within any other community.

First, how do you dress your protective services staff? That is, what *uniforms* will they wear? In an educational environment such as a college or university, it may not draw unwanted attention to have SWAT-style personnel roaming around, even if activated merely for training perhaps. Any panic arising from the population would likely be centered on the perception that something "wrong" was undertaken. Of course, the observation of other students going about his or her day might lessen this fear.

In a medical facility such as a hospital, however, greater care must be given to the patient population. Suppose, for example, there were combat veterans present. Such sights may cause them grief if it brought up post-traumatic stress syndrome (PTSD) issues. The same would apply for victims of violent crime.

For these reasons alone, your healthcare security personnel should emulate the more formal attire of executive protection personnel (see Figure 26). These personnel could wear body armor (bulletproof vests) and carry .45 caliber handguns with no pedestrians noticing their role as security. Larger individuals could even sport short-barreled rifles in shoulder harnesses should the prospects for terrorist attacks arise. In most cases, however, *a well-trained* and *practiced* shooter will dispense with active shooters and homicide bombers.

Figure 26. Security subdued...and unleashed. © a4stockphotos - Fotolia.com (L), © poco_bw - Fotolia.com (R).

Second, how *will* you arm your personnel? Remember, security without firearms equals servants without respect. An armed aggressor will not obey your receptionist any more than a patient with a kidney stone will listen to a Red Cross volunteer. Your community will have to face this reality; otherwise, a great many people are going to die...eventually. It may take a hundred years or, perhaps, a hundred hours, but are *you* willing to place patient and staff lives on the line through such a gamble?

The most effective concealed firearm remains a tactical pistol in .45 ACP caliber (see Figure 15). With magazines carrying 8 to 13 rounds each, such a firearm provides the security professional with a range of options, spanning from frangible ammunition (most appropriate for healthcare settings), to hollow points (designed to inflict the most damage upon tissue) to full-metal jacket rounds (comparatively inexpensive for range training). Many tactical-type .45s also possess threaded barrels for shooters to affix suppressors, which are legal in many states providing that the purchaser pays the federal transfer tax. These aid in training as well as certain operational duties.

Because the .45 ACP represents a large, slow moving bullet, it does not exceed the speed of sound. Combined with a suppressor, therefore, firearm discharges involve very little noise. At least nothing, that would, say, disturb patients in the next room. This brings us to discussing the third major concern – *where* to conduct such security training?

Many hospitals maintain disused corridors and wings that, for a variety of reasons, no longer match the profit expectations or services offered by the facility owner. These portions of the hospital can be used for staging incident response simulations and, even, red team exercises. Depending upon the location, legalities, and liabilities, such disused portions of the hospital can be readily set up to conduct live-fire exercises (the technical aspects are sound, but municipalities tend to frown upon *anything* involving firearms). At a minimum, they are equally suited for dry run training with actual "shots fired" scenarios left to many of the larger firearms ranges scattered around the nation.

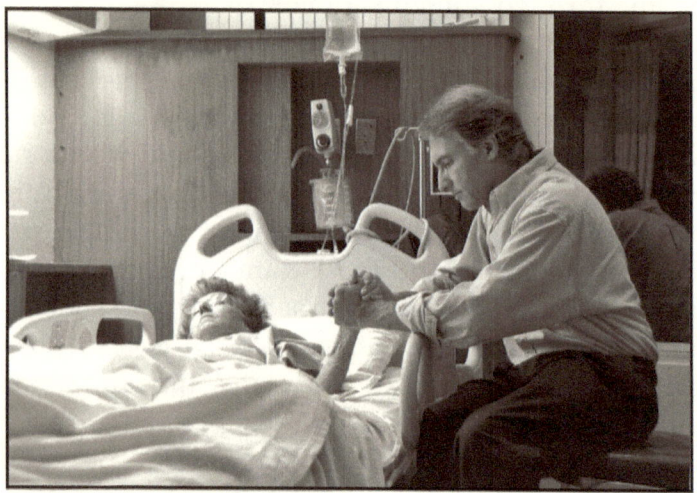

Figure 27. Understanding the environment. © Claudio's Pics - Fotolia.com

The final primary concern with establishing your security plan rests with the realization of the environment that your people will be operating within (see Figure 27). Whether major public hospital or the most exclusive specialty client, yours represents a setting where people remain at their most vulnerable condition. Fear, anxiety, depression, anger, and denial represent some of the conflicting emotions that swirl through your environment, sometimes alone and often in various combinations. No one entering a hospital is going to be as excited as a freshman college student or another reaching graduation.

At best, the most elated people in *any* healthcare facility are going to be the proud parents of a newborn infant. Even then, however, one or both parents will be extremely agitated over the care given to their son or daughter. For your role, you will have to accept the inherent unease of everyone located within your area of responsibility. That doctor, for instance, that you joke to nearly every day of the week may have just lost a patient. Perhaps the nurse near whose desk you stop for a coffee has had to deal with an elderly patient whose mannerisms have long passed into senility.

Nobody likes to visit a hospital and few prefer to work there. Yet, you have *consciously chosen* the healthcare profession for undoubtedly several personal reasons. However you ended up within your particular community – money, prestige, compassion, an opportunity to be a servant – you hold possession of that "grave duty" to protect those under your care. Inasmuch as a physician bears responsibility to diagnosis correctly and a nurse exerts loyalty towards the patient he or she is administering medication to, your fundamental obligation rests with doing everything humanly possible to save the lives of those individuals who may come under threat.

For the 21st century, such aggression may come in the form of a computer hacker attempting to murder a prominent patient from the other side of the planet through tinkering with that person's medication record.[46] At the other end of the spectrum, a street gang may enter the premises to finish killing a

---

[46] Douglas Schweitzer, *Securing the Network from Malicious Code: A Complete Guide to Defending Against Viruses, Worms, and Trojans* (Indianapolis: Wiley Publishing, 2002), 217.

wounded police officer and his wife.[47] Whatever the
case may represent, your community now represents a
society at war.

You may absolutely *fear* the presence of armed
security professionals within your particular facility,
but you no longer bear the choice for jihadist terrorists
and narco-traffickers have *already* declared war upon
you and your community – and they are steadily
destroying hospitals and healthcare facilities around
the world. Not to mention the millions of patients their
actions affect.

Long gone are the days when the mere sighting
of a red cross would divert the aggression of national
armies; today's belligerents represent little more than
thugs whose primary concern involves profit – or
prophet. As long as you do not obey them, cater to his
or her wishes, or simply belong to an offensive group,
they *will* target you for destruction. *Wherever* you live
or work.

---

[47] Memorandum for the record, as had happened with a friend of the
author's sister, circa 1970s/1980s.

15. HARDENING THE HOLY

DURING the year 1220, Genghis Khan stood within the mosque of Bukhara and declared to the Muslims present that he represented "...the punishment of God" for the great sins they had allegedly committed.[48] Perhaps such an outrage would have infuriated the residents of Bukhara more had not their own holy prophet employed mosques as "a place to store weapons and make military plans."[49]

This remains true to principle for a religious figure who militarily "planned sixty-five campaigns and raids, and personally led twenty-seven."[50] As a Christian hemisphere, the West has largely excluded religion from warfare, as it has since banned religious faith from everywhere but within the confines of an individual's mind. It therefore seems odd, that under the context of so much hostility towards persons of faith, that we should remain aghast over the thought that our places of worship have come exceedingly under attack during the 21st century.

---

[48] Timothy May, *The Mongol Art of War: Chinggis Khan and the Mongol Military System* (Yardley, PA: Westholme Publishing, 2007), 7.
[49] Mark A. Gabriel, *Islam and Terrorism: What the Quran Really Teaches About Christianity, Violence, and the Goals of the Islamic Jihad* (Lake Mary, FL: Charisma House, 2002), 97-100.

Nevertheless, the mere concept of religion suggests that one person's beliefs must remain far superior to another's, for to *believe* indicates full and unconditional allegiance to a set of ideas, values, and codes of conduct. Otherwise, an individual would immediately fall into the trap of mere "thinking".

These differences of belief can be reviewed in context of the three major monotheistic religions (discussed for their belief within the same God): Judaism, Christianity, and Islam. Judaism introduces the concept of a Chosen People by a singular God. Christianity believes that that "one God" so loved the world, that he came amongst his people and suffered the same indignities that have plagued people for centuries so that his followers might find eternal life. Islam, for its role, suggests that the first two groups had so violated their beliefs that *another* prophet had to appear to set the record straight.

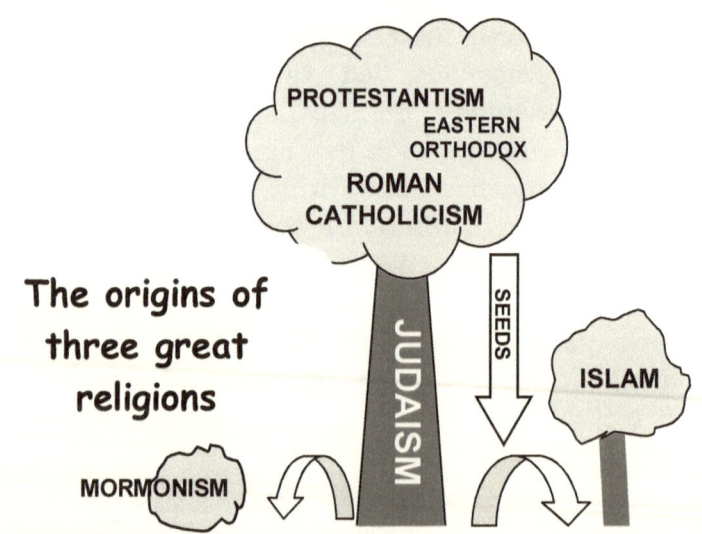

Figure 28. The origins of Judaism, Christianity, and Islam.

[50] Will Durant, *The Age of Faith* (New York: Simon and Schuster, 1950),

As can be observed within Figure 28, all three religious faiths sprouted from the same seed. Nevertheless, whereas Christianity rests upon the tree trunk of Judaism, Islam represents an entirely different rooting, a doctrine heavily influenced by Judaism flavored with the views of several Christian sects that were considered heretical by the Church.[51] This provides us with a platform upon which to gauge modern views of religious facilities.

Judaism retains its historical, Zionist views of Jerusalem representing the ancestral capital of the "Chosen People" and, thus, centers interests upon the remains of the Temple of Solomon, etc. Christianity removes this adherence to "physical" locations and fixtures and refocuses the adherent to *living* a life based upon the Gospel tradition of its founder. Islam, basically, fuses both beliefs and seeks to obtain a global government under Allah (God), for which territorial possessions and sacred sites remain a pillar upon which to cement humans' relation with their deity. Each religious belief thus purports to represent the one, *true* Way.

Politically, however, both Judaic and Islamic aggressions during the present can be traced back to succession rights of the first born of Abraham.[52] As an inclusive faith based upon forgiveness and tolerance, Christianity sheds the physical for the spiritual and

---

170.
[51] Ibid., 184-186.
[52] The present Arab-Israeli conflict can be attributed to succession rights regarding Abraham's firstborn son, Ishmael (conceived through slave Hagar), and his second born Isaac (conceived through wife Sarah) and representing Arabs and Jews respectively. See Anthony M. Davis, *Terrorism and the Maritime Transportation System: Are We on a Collision Course?*(Livermore, CA: WingSpan Press, 2008), 16-17.

attempts to gain adherents through acceptance of believers from all nationalities, races, and social positions. Its concept of "Repay to Caesar what belongs to Caesar…" suggests that Christians must accept earthly authority to a point.[53]

For American readers, the beliefs of Islam remain little different from the more local ideas of the Church of Jesus Christ of Latter-day Saints, or Mormons. Both Islam and Mormonism were established by an individual who believed to receive a "new" revelation that superseded the Bible, that their new book (the Quran and Book of Mormon, respectively) represented this *final* revelation from God. That both founders received his 'revelation' directly from a spiritual being and that this particular "angel" actually transcribed the book for them.

Thus far, we have discussed the beliefs of a few religions rather than the houses where believers practice his or her faith. This was intended to show the reader the baseline beliefs that *may* cause animosity towards persons of another faith. Nevertheless, the discussion also suggests a reason for why individuals have, historically, offered little in the way of security for holy places – Westerners, particularly Americans, believe that religion represents peace and tranquility whereas most of the world views religion as *conquest* to enslave non-believers.

If, for instance, Muhammad employed mosques, as command centers for waging war, then it must be accepted that the most fanatical (factual?) adherents to the Muhammadan spirit of Islam suspect that *other* houses of worship are similarly used. This represents the practice of 'mirror imaging' that confronts

---

[53] Mark 12:17, *New American Bible*.

intelligence professionals – the practice of superimposing one's beliefs and cultures upon others. That is, "We believe that *we* would do this if we *were them...*" Or else, in more colloquial thought, "If *I* had all their money, I *would do...*"

Muhammad used mosques for war so, therefore, Muslims must consider that Christians *also* use churches for wars against Islam. Conversely, mirror imaging suggests to Christians that since churches are holy and their use for conflict represents a great sin, then so, too, must it be a sin to employ mosques to store weapons and orchestrate battles. Both sides misunderstand one another's beliefs and this leads to conflicts throughout the world. It also explains why fanatical Muslims (arguably, those *truest* to Muhammadan traditions) seek to destroy Christian churches and holy sites around the world. One only needs to grasp history and see where once powerful Christian sites have stood (i.e, Constantinople, etc.), there now remain few of any Christians allowed to practice.

If one group of individuals believes that the true mark of victory remains to abolish the beliefs and history of another, then it can be assumed that more groups exist that share this philosophy. Russia, as but one example, tried to squash Polish culture during its past occupation of that nation, going as far as to attempt to abolish its Roman Catholicism, which remains very similar to Russian Orthodoxy. Moscow forced Poles to sneak to church through city sewers simply because Russia could not accept a competitive Christian doctrine.

Again, elsewhere in the world churches and other religious facilities are viewed with contempt offering Americans and, perhaps, others insight into security related issues regarding these unique environments. The Charleston shooting discussed in Chapter 7 merely affirmed this shift away from naiveté: the United States is no longer immune to beheadings, church shootings, or being murdered simply for who someone is – *all* these things having occurred during the past few years.

Now, the question rests, if churches are under attack, who is to say that *only* churches will be attacked? The truth remains, inasmuch as educational institutions and healthcare facilities are targeted, so too are places of worship irrespective of faith. To conclude that churches are inherently "special" and do not require proactive security provisions remains an absurd concept.

	Church	Mosque	Synagogue
Active Shooter	6	5	6
Suicide Bomber	5	4	7
Political Protest	6	8	9
Deranged Individual	6	7	8

Figure 29. Threat matrix for religious facilities.

The threat probability matrix for religious facilities remains a little different from that for schools and hospitals, since religious affiliated members of those two groups are classified along with the secular institutions. In this regard, we have remained with the most probable threats as other disturbances such as fire, weather, power outages, etc. remain negligible for smaller structures.

We have also assumed that the relatively few

mosques within countries such as the United States (0.6% Muslim versus ~75% Christian) retain higher threat probabilities due to social issues and the consideration that recent Muslim immigrants have not had sufficient time to assimilate.

Figure 30. Interior entrance to a large church. ©2011 R.J. Godlewski

Figure 31. Interior side of large church. ©2011 R.J. Godlewski

In Figures 30 and 31, we observe the interior portion of a larger Midwestern church facing towards the altar at the end of the aisle (Figure 30). Aside from the extraordinary replacement value of this early 20th century structure, the reader can foresee significant issues with security, particularly if aggressors confront a distracted congregation. The number of pews that parishioners would have to vacate would hamper egress from the church.

Furthermore, the age of the church suggests that pews remain too close to one another to offer effective protection; only those fortunate enough to lay down *on* a pew could secure themselves, the floor remaining an option for only the slightest of frames. The ornamentation and pillars may offer protection against bullets, but they also prevent safe passage or, perhaps, even recognition of victims or casualties.

Figure 32. The rear of the church in Figures 30 and 31.
©2011 R.J. Godlewski

As with most older churches, especially many within the southern United States that changed hands frequently between denominations, there exists a upper level used either for extra seating or musical choirs (see Figure 32). This arrangement offers several concerns for security personnel:

- How does security access the upper level without tipping off their presence should an active shooter or suicide bomber exist within that particular location?

- Can this upper level be evacuated should a shooting or bombing occur on the first floor?

- What advantages exist if security is placed in the upper level?

In consideration of these concerns, it is recommended that churches place only choirs and other staff positions, insofar as possible, within the upper level to prevent casualties amongst the public.

Secondly, it is advised to staff security personnel – even if only "volunteer" ushers – in the upper level with radios and, perhaps, binoculars so that he or she would be able to use the height advantage to peer down upon the congregation, seeking suspicious activity that suggest diversion from religious services. As with a coaching staff during a football game or spotters during an auto race, these personnel will be able to direct traffic below should an incident occur.

Finally, with the upper level restricted to only choirs, etc., it may be advised to shield them with curtains, instruments, etc. so that persons with ill intent may not be able to observe the mezzanine with any degree of effectiveness. Your community should always retain tactical advantage, even if your building represents a small, one-room facility.

That churches employ ushers permits them to move personnel around without a great deal of attention by the congregation and any members therein. Even should a probable active shooter detect their presence, he or she cannot keep observing all ushers. Therefore, such scrutiny of a congregation should always be employed through teams of ushers and other personnel.

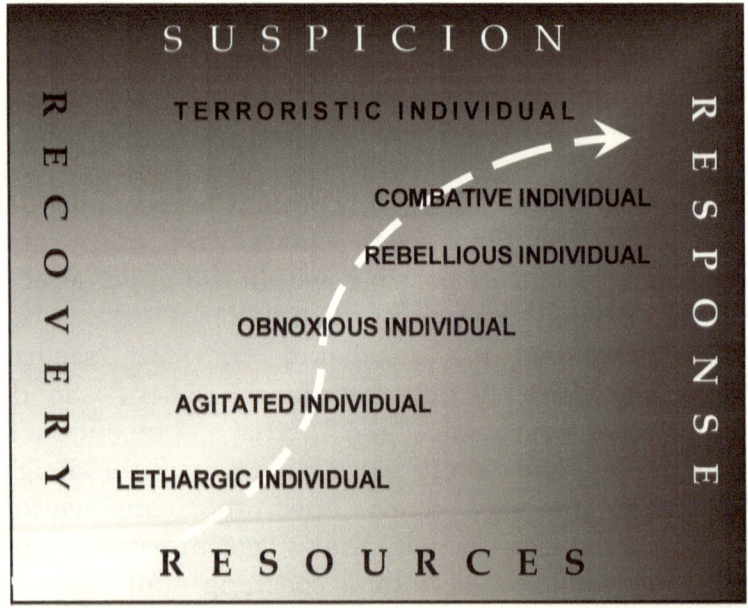

Figure 33. Scaling suspicion.

In Figure 33, we observe the relationship between suspicion, response, resources, and recovery when dealing with a host of questionable individuals.

In this graphic, we observe that a lethargic individual (possibly one experiencing lack of sleep or pending heart attack) does not appear overly suspicious nor does he or she require a significant response. As such, community staff should observe this individual in case he or she does require subsequent medical attention. For this reason, such an individual does not pull ushers or other personnel *away* from an opportunity to "recover" back to standard operating mode.

An obnoxious individual, however, rests within the middle of the graphic indicating that he or she bears upon the most inflexible scenario. He or she pulls resources away from staff, but does not yet require a significant response. They are certainly suspicious, but do not cross the "point of no return" that tips the scale. In other words, *even* obnoxious individuals can cease being burdensome.

On the far end of the scale, of course, we come across the terroristic individual whose actions both preclude any trust and demand unconditional response from facility staff. Such an individual draws the most resources (security, etc.) away from other duties and prevents an easy return to normalcy once their character is made known.

From this chart, we can analyze several potential responses regarding each type of individual:

- *Lethargic Individuals.* An individual may be lethargic or drowsy for any number of reasons. Perhaps he or she had just finished a long shift at work or, maybe, a baby kept them awake during the night. Nothing in their actions suggests that they may be a threat to anyone. That said, their condition might hint at a medical problem. Therefore, ushers and other concerned persons should pay attention to them and if the situation warrants, offer a word or two of support in case there may exist an underlying physiological ailment.

- *Agitated Individuals.* These individuals are excited about *something* or through some *condition.* Perhaps he or she received a speeding ticket on the way to services. They may also be suffering from the effects of medication or the weather (e.g., asthmatic persons, etc.). He or she must be observed in order that their anxiety does not propel their condition further along.

- *Obnoxious Individuals.* An obnoxious person represents an agitated soul whose inhibitions have exhausted. They are simply frustrated and want the world to suffer along with them. These persons must be dealt with immediately and diplomatically or else he or she will turn other individuals into agitated persons. However, if they do not respond to suggestion, their presence should be notified to local law enforcement as his or her condition does not mandate the involvement of limited security resources.

- *Rebellious Individuals.* These represent individuals that choose to pick a fight and care less about the ruckus he or she makes. They remain limited in physicality, but this does not make him or her easier to work with. In fact, such an individual may actually be *seeking* physical response from your community in order to escalate the situation for advantage. If your community holds any police officers or attorneys within its congregation, they should be recruited as witnesses should security have to escort the individual outside until active law enforcement personnel arrive.

- *Combative Individuals.* Combative individuals represent a significant escalation in threats, since he or she has reacted *physically* to any pleas for peace and submission. They must be removed from the vicinity and turned over to proper authority. Should they present an immediate threat to other individuals, however, security personnel must exercise force to subdue them as appropriate.

- *Terroristic Individuals.* When any individual's desire to turn physical action into sheer terror of his or her surroundings, be they an active shooter, suicide bomber, or knife-wielding psychopath, their function remains to spread terror amongst your community. They must be subdued as quickly and efficiently as possible, even if this means employing immediate lethal force. Your security personnel (and community staff) cannot allow for police response times.

The reaction of security personnel towards the above scaling threats must be seamless and procedural. There can be no hesitation, for instance, if the simply lethargic individual turns out to be under the influence of narcotics and rapidly escalates through obnoxious, combative, and, possibly terroristic categories within a few brief minutes.

That churches, synagogues, and mosques are now considered legitimate targets for anyone with a grievance or hatred is proven through a simple review of the news. Not only have they suffered thievery, burglary, vandalism, and bigotry for decades, active shooters, bombings, and sabotage have turned raw disgust into absolute hatred.

No matter the size of your particular religious community, you have seen your share of primal human aggression. Perhaps, your sensibilities have prevented you from calling any of the above incidences as "aggression", but anytime someone forces you to undertake a thought, action, or response, they have effectively become an aggressor. Yours may be a peaceful community, but that only makes it an oasis within a world full of wolves. Flocks must be protected with sheepdogs – not lapdogs.

> *"Your servant used to tend his father's sheep, and whenever a lion or bear came to carry off a sheep from the flock, I would go after it and attack it and rescue the prey from its mouth. If it attacked me, I would seize it by the jaw, strike it, and kill it."*[54] David to King Saul.

---

[54] 1 Samuel 17:34-35, *NAB*.

16. *FUTURUM EXSPECTAT*

THROUGHOUT this book, we have traveled through a discussion on protecting your community, whether that particular community represented a school or university, hospital or healthcare clinic, synagogue or church. In these previous fifteen chapters, our journey brought about suggestions, realizations, and, perhaps, hopes for the members of your organization.

This pilgrimage took you through the basis of human value and survival, turned the course at defense and martial tactics, and led you into consideration of war and the many resources necessary to wage it successfully. What this informational trip was not, however, was a vacation. It required you to shatter your preconceived notions about safety in such communal places as universities and hospitals. It taught you that churches, synagogues, and mosques were *not* under the exclusive care of God; that we all bear our responsibilities in aiding Him to affect our own security.

Some individuals may argue over the structure or even target audience of this book, but rarely do ordinary people learn through the 'textbook' approach. Nor is knowledge gained simply by looking up the answers through an index or electronic search. For this reason, *Communities at War* exists within an evolving format, offering the reader an opportunity to discover about his or her community through suggestions provided for other institutions.

To defend against primal aggression requires an individual to build his or her repertoire of mechanisms for such defense. This requires continually gaining and applying subsequent information until *response* becomes second nature. One, therefore, cannot always rely upon *Kata* for conditioning. When you reach desire, you will retain and when you retain, you will learn.

Of course, you are reading this book because you realize that the modern world is becoming rather archaically dangerous and violent. Perhaps it was just a spontaneous declaration of curiosity on your part, but you would not have made it this far along if you simply wanted to learn the fastest way to die (hint: it involves stagnation).

A wise and anonymous man once declared that the two most important days of your life involved the day that you were born and the one where you realized why. You may now include a third: the day when you finally decided that you were going to *survive* come hell or high water. And because your fight to survive takes you through numerous communities of diverse persons, you correctly assumed that *your* survival often rests upon the shoulders of *others*.

You may not always feel comfortable with it, but even the best-trained warrior may succumb to defeat if his supporting cast is weak. Therefore, you have decided to take matters into your own hands and *force* your community into sharing responsibility for *everyone's* survival. At least as much of that "everyone" as you can reasonably influence.

This will not be easy – yet simpler than dying an aggravating death – for your institution remains populated with a great many individuals who take survival for granted or place it fully into the hands of others. With which option would *you* feel most comfortable? To aid within this decision, place your bank account into the hands of a total stranger and see if luck rests with you. Of course, you can *always* replenish a savings or checking account. Extinguishing your life through ignorance is inexcusable, especially if you take a great many people along for the ride.

Within this text, we have focused upon three communities that require a compassionate shove in order to think about safety and survival. These represent educational institutions, healthcare facilities, and houses of worship. That they teach, heal, and inspire seems to matter very little to those that populate them. In fact, it may be argued that society's most vulnerable institutions exist because society has failed to adequately protect its greatest treasures.

As with a thief in the night, we have slowly capitulated to those who hold no such limitations on where or how he or she seeks to destroy that treasure. We give away civilization, because we are far too weak to retain it. We have become quitters – effectively ceasing work upon the stroke of the clock, living upon the arrival of pension checks, and surrendering upon the sight of an intruder. *Why?*

Does not our heart beat after our departure from work? Do we see any less when we retire? Have our ears abandoned their function when terror strikes? Thinking back upon your life, has that most terrible of memories prevented you from reading these words? Of course not.

General George Patton once declared that he did not judge anyone by how high he or she climbed, but by how high that individual bounced whenever he or she hit bottom. Our society seems to have struck bottom and the rebound is up for grabs. We no longer seem to value human life, even that of our most vulnerable unborn. We no longer respect those who place their lives on the line so that the rest of society may go about disinterested about others. For the "*One nation, under God*" whose own declaration of independence held such "*truths to be self-evident, that all men are created equal, that they are endowed by their Creator with certain unalienable Rights, that among these are Life, Liberty and the pursuit of Happiness*", we have effectively placed that Great Power in a closet never to be released again.

Is it really any wonder, then, why our schools, hospitals, and houses of God remain targeted? Can we expect less than to have our innocent children slaughtered at the hands of Evil? When others come to reduce our unalienable rights, can we expect *not* to relinquish them? What future does society possess if to progress requires abandoning our standing firm and voicing our opinions?

Evil places these questions into our minds, often indiscreetly and enticingly. For it is pleasurable to refrain from responsibility, dignity, and honor. To do as we wish and avoid compassion towards fellow human beings. In the immortal words of Edmund Burke, this Evil succeeds because we do *nothing*. If we only lifted a finger to say "Enough! Your destruction ends *here*", how many lives could be saved?

Yet, few bother to lift that finger. We observe on

television retail shoppers step over the body of a beaten neighbor without gazing down. We hear public officials tell police to step aside and permit thuggery to escalate. We see politicians employ tragedy merely to affect his or her agenda. All over the world, we hear the voices of the vanquished and the oppressed cry out for freedom and, yet, the United Nations focuses upon so-called "Climate Change" as if a temperature degree or two a thousand years from now is more important than human life today.

If we do not change the stance on defending our communities during the present, we will not survive long enough to worry about the weather tomorrow. Yes, the future matters; *our* future. Without humanity around to experience it, the natural world matters little in the greater scheme of Creation.

Civilization must survive upon three foundations – how we broaden our knowledge, how we restore our vigor, and how we save our souls. The ignorant and confused cannot create. The fragile and obese cannot respond. And the scandalous cannot endure.

Accordingly, we must defend our schools and universities from those who wish to kill and indoctrinate, our hospitals from those who wish to destroy and infect, and our places of worship from those who wish to contaminate and transgress. Neither will be easy. Neither will be popular. Nothing good ever is.

The 21st century is, without a doubt, the great "undiscovered country". The potential for the human race remains extraordinarily great, as a mere glance at the past one hundred years suggests. Conversely, it may be as hazardous as the first half of the 20th century. Much depends upon how we approach it and how we define it. Do we fight for our survival? Or do we simply acquiesce to "public authority" and abandon our responsibility for empowering that public authority. Tyranny is but inaction away.

The most difficult task, perhaps, rests with securing our schools, colleges, and universities. On the one hand, these represent open and free spaces where diverse groups come to interact and exchange ideas in order to learn from one another and develop personal intuitions and creativity. This makes them susceptible to visitors with ill intent – an unlocked door will always be opened. On the other hand, colleges and universities, in particular, represent establishments where spiritual dissent is challenged and religious liberties and the sanctity of human life much frowned upon.

This duplicity ensures that aggressors are protected and defenders ostracized. Nevertheless, as human beings we are morally bound to defend other human beings despite the Darwinian law that dictates that like-species will always compete for supremacy. Such institutions may not like the concept of a God, for instance, but the alternative remains hellish.

Therefore, to protect our educational institutions properly requires an absolute approach, one that is not extinguished by the calendar or committee, liability or legislation. Only when individuals are safe can debate begin. Only when we breathe can we truly *live*. And only when we truly *defend*, can we survive.

Healthcare facilities rest a close second when the difficulty to protect remains considered. Like colleges and universities, they attract a wide variety of visitors and residents, not all of which bear a definite need to be on site. Unlike schools, however, hospitals and other healthcare facilities house the most vulnerable of a nation's citizenry – newborn infants, expectant mothers, people with injuries or illnesses, and the elderly. Specialist institutions care for the addicted and the unstable. This diversity requires protection a magnitude more reflective than, perhaps, engaging an active shooter on campus.

Hospitals not only possess the vulnerable, they contain vast quantities of dangerous chemicals and compounds, miles of industrial piping and technology, and permit vehicular and aircraft traffic unheard of for such a congested area. All these things make healthcare facilities singularly dangerous for response units engaging aggressive individuals. Most college campuses are, for comparison, spread wide amongst hundreds of acres. Not so for hospitals, which in the West often remain interconnected with corridors and attached outbuildings.

Churches, synagogues, and mosques rounded out our discussion of unique places to defend. On one level, they share the same personnel, equipment, and tactical considerations as schools and hospitals, which is why neither of the groups explored were presented within "standalone" discussion entirely.

Unfortunately, religious institutions, particularly those subscribing to Abrahamic monotheism, bear a singularly problematic consideration: everyone expects *God* to protect his or her life, especially within such houses of worship. Few bother to consider that, perhaps, God uses *people* to do His bidding. That is, God is not likely to render aid as long as there are hundreds, perhaps even thousands, of believers within the congregation. When a doctor heals, for instance, such success usually rests upon the shoulders of a great many nurses, laboratory workers, therapists, etc.

To survive within these environments requires a great deal of effort on the part of those who want to *live*. We cannot rely upon the concept of *others*, for the primary reason that "others" will not always be available when needed. After all, *who* travels wherever you do, experiences everything you experience, and shares every thought as you other than yourself?

Defending our communities requires people to accept the simultaneous roles of warrior, educator, and servant all rolled into one compassionate and responsible individual. This is *not* the same as serving as judge, jury, and executioner. We cannot judge, act with more information than most juries possess, and only – repeat *ONLY* – serve as executioners so that others may live. To kill remains the greatest failure of any security detail.

Nevertheless, individuals are often required to do things that he or she prefers not to do. For instance, few college students prefer to study for complicated calculus exams. Few physicians prefer to slice into a human body. Few priests and ministers care to attend a funeral. Yet, each of these activities epitomize the role of that particular individual, whether student, doctor, or pastor.

Similarly, security represents a function whose purpose may involve things that *no* human is prepared to undertake. Conversely, soldiers, even if only at the most subconscious level, foresee a future where he or she may have to engage within combat to carry out his or her function dutifully. Police officers may never fire his or her gun on the job, but they remain trained to do so nonetheless.

While security professionals work diligently to protect through deterrence, he or she may not escape the situation where lethal force is required. Most, assuredly, would prefer to walk the quiet halls of a school or hospital, joke with friendly coworkers or, perhaps, extend an inspiring word or two to a patient or student. After all, security professionals remain *human* as with all other individuals.

The world is not populated exclusively with friendly coworkers, for many seek to harm others as with the individual down in Oklahoma who beheaded one person and proceeded to behead another before he was subdued. Nor does it represent a community where all patients are injured or sick due to outside influences. Finally, the global community of students is not entirely academic, as the 9/11 hijackers proved beyond all doubt.

Security personnel – whether professional or volunteer – must *always* remember that a full *sixty-five* percent of those they encounter can inflict lethal force with little prompting. It matters little whether that population consists of students or educators, physicians or patients, clerics or laity. *Every* person on planet earth bears the capacity to kill. Some merely prefer to do so to save others.

These honorable individuals, many but not all populating Western military forces, need emulation. Protectors are those who endorse the dignity and integrity of *all human persons* without regard to his or her nationality, religious faith, social status, or financial position. To discriminate suggests bigotry; to segregate suggests tyranny. Both remain confrontational towards human survival.

Security professionals are, at the very least, professionals whose function is, again, to protect and defend. They do not necessarily uphold the law as with police officers or do they wage war as with the military.

They do not heal as with physicians, though he or she may teach. Certainly, protective services professionals do not entertain the enlightenment of the soul despite their occasional involvement with separating that soul from its body.

The world of professional security remains universal and borderless. It exists to ensure that people remain free to exercise those unalienable rights that the United States of America so proudly declared for all posterity. It represents less of a job than a 'Way', to borrow that martial term from Asia. However it may be termed, security professionals serve to protect human individuals by "any means necessary".

It matters little whether your community represents an educational institution, a healthcare facility, or a house of God; if you do not protect your life and those of your members, someone will eventually *take* that life from you. Your job is to prolong that eventuality for as long as humanly possible. You must exist to "render the aggressor unable to inflict harm." *Period.*

RECOMMENDED READING

AbuKhalil, A. (2005). Arab-Israeli Conflict. In C. Press, *The Middle East* (Tenth Edition ed., pp. 13-78). Washington: CQ Press.

Akhavan, J. (2006). *The Chemistry of Explosives* (Second Edition ed.). Cambridge, England: Royal Society of Chemistry.

Aloise, G. (2007, November 15). COMBATING NUCLEAR TERRORISM: Federal Efforts to Respond to Nuclear and Radiological Threats and to Protect Key Emergency Response Facilities Could Be Strengthened. (t. F. Subcommittee on Oversight of Government Management, Interviewer) U.S. Government Accountability Office.

al-Qaeda. (n.d.). Declaration of Jihad (Holy War) Against the Country's Tyrants, Military Series.

Andrew, C., & Mitrokhin, V. (1999). *The Sword and the Shield: The Mitrokhin Archive and the Secret History of the KGB*. New York: Basic Books.

Argonne National Laboratory. (2005). *Radiological Disperal Device (RDD)*. Chicago: Argonne National Laboratory.

Arias, E. D. (2010). Understanding Criminal Networks, Political Order, and Politics in Latin America. In A. L. Clunan, & H. A. Trinkunas (Eds.), *Ungoverned Spaces: Alternatives to State Authority in an Era of Softened Sovereignty* (pp. 115-135). Stanford, CA: Stanford Security Studies/Stanford University Press.

Aslan, R. (2006). *No god but God: The Origins, Evolution, and Future of Islam.* New York: Random House.

Baer, R. (2002). *See No Evil: The True Story of a Ground Soldier in the CIA's War on Terrorism.* New York: Three Rivers Press.

Baer, R. (2010, April). *Politics: GQ.* Retrieved April 17, 2010, from GQ Magazine Web site: http://www.gq.com/news-politics/politics/201004/dagger-to-the-cia

Bailey, B. J., & Bailey, J. M. (2003). *Who Are the Christians in the Middle East?* Grand Rapids, MI: William B. Eerdmans Publishing Company.

Balor, P. (1988). *Manual of the Mercenary Soldier.* Boulder: Paladin Press.

Beevor, A. (1998). *Stalingrad: The Fateful Siege: 1942-1943.* New York: Penguin Books.

Bejtlich, R. (2011, February 2). *Cooking the Cuckoo's Egg.* Retrieved December 13, 2012, from Tao Security Website: http://www.taosecurity.com/bejtlich_doj_cooking_06feb11a.pdf

Bergman, R. (2010, August 5). Hezbollah and the Lebanon Dilemma. *Wall Street Journal (Eastern edition),* p. A17.

Bernstein, P. I. (2006). *Weapons of Mass Destruction: A Primer.* Advanced Systems and Concepts Office. Washington: Defense Threat Reduction Agency.

Biddle, S., & Friedman, J. A. (2008). *THE 2006 LEBANON CAMPAIGN AND THE FUTURE OF WARFARE: Implications for Army and Defense Policy.* Carlisle, PA: Strategic Studies Institute.

Black, I., & Morris, B. (1991). *Israel's Secret Wars: A History of Israel's Intelligence Services.* New York: Grove Press.

Bodansky, Y. (1994). *TERROR! The inside story of the terrorist conspiracy in America.* SPI Books.

Bodansky, Y. (2007). *Chechen Jihad: Al-Qaeda's Training Ground and the Next Wave of Terror.* New York: Harper.

Bodansky, Y. (n.d.). CHECHNYA: The Mujahedin Factor. Retrieved September 19, 2012, from http://www.freeman.org/m_online/bodansky/c hechnya.htm

Bowden, M. (2001). *Killing Pablo: The Hunt for the World's Greatest Outlaw.* New York: Penguin Books.

Brands, H. (2009). *Mexico's Narco-Insurgency and U.S. Counterdrug Policy.* Carlisle, PA: Strategic Studies Institute.

Brands, H. (2010). *Crime, Violence, and the Crisis in Guatemala: A Case Study in the Erosion of the State.* Carlisle: Strategic Studies Institute.

Byman, D. (2005). *Deadly Connections: States that Sponsor Terrorism.* New York: Cambridge University Press.

Celeski, J. D. (2010). *Hunter-Killer Teams: Attacking Enemy Safe Havens.* Hurlburt Field: Joint Special Operations University.

Chinn, K.-l. (1996). *Chinatown Gangs: Extortion, Enterprise, & Ethnicity.* New York: Oxford University Press.

Clark, R. M. (2007). *Intelligence Analysis: A target-centric approach.* Washington: CQ Press.

Clarke, R. A., & Knake, R. K. (2010). *Cyber War: The Next Threat to National Security and What to Do about It.* New York: Harper Collins/Ecco.

Clausewitz, C. v. (1984). *On War.* (M. H. Paret, Trans.) Princeton: Princeton University Press.

Coll, S. (2004). *Ghost Wars: The Secret History of the CIA, Afghanistan, and Bin Laden, from the Soviet Invasion to Steptember 10, 2001.* New York: Penguin Books.

Colling, R. L., & York, T. W. (2010). *Hospital and Healtchare Security* (5th Edition ed.). Burlington, MA: Elsevier.

Couch, D. (2010). *A Tactical Ethic: Moral Conduct in the Insurgent Battlespace.* Annapolis, MD: Naval Institute Press.

Cox, R. (1983). Total Terrorism: Argentina, 1969 to 1979. In M. Crenshaw, *Terrorism, Legitimacy, and Power* (pp. 124-142). Middletown, CT: Wesleyan.

Cragin, K., & Hoffman, B. (2003). *Arms Trafficking and Colombia.* Santa Monica, CA: RAND Corporation.

Cwiek, M. A. (2005). America after 9/11. In G. R. Ledlow, J. A. Johnson, & W. J. Jones (Eds.), *Community Preparedness and Response to Terrorism: The Terrorist Threat and Community Response* (Vol. I, pp. 7-21). Westport, Connecticut: Praeger.

Dashti, A. (1994). *Twenty Three Years: A study of the Prophetic Career of Mohammad.*

Dauber, C. I. (2009). *YouTube War: Fighting in a World of Cameras in every Cell Phone and Photoshop on every Computer.* Carlisle, PA: Strategic Studies Institute.

Dawson, R. (1986). The Secrets of Power Negotiating. Chicago.

de Wijze, S. (2009, September). Targeted killing: a 'dirty hands' analysis. *Contemporary Politics, 15*(3), 305-320.

Decker, S. H., & Chapman, M. T. (2008). *Drug Smugglers on Drug Smuggling: Lessons from the Inside.* Philadelphia: Temple University Press.

Department of the Army. (2005). *FM 3-05.30 PSYCHOLOGICAL OPERATIONS.* Washington: United States Government.

Dewar, M. (1992). *War in the Streets: The Story of Urban Combat from Calais to Khafji.* London: David & Charles.

Dobson, C., & Payne, R. (1982). *Counterattack: The West's battle against the terrorists.* New York: Facts on File, Inc.

Donnelly, T. (2006, October). A Question of Faith: Conflicts Driven by Religion Can be Long and Bitter. *Armed Forces Journal,* pp. 60-62.

Dreyfuss, M. (2012, January). My Fellow Americans, We Are Going to Kill You: The Legality of Targeting and Killing U.S. Citizens Abroad. *Vanderbilt Law Review, 65*(1), 249-292.

Durant, W. (1950). *The Age of Faith.* New York: Simon and Schuster.

Dzikansky, M., Kleiman, G., & Slater, R. (2012). *Terrorist Suicide Bombings: Attack Interdiction, Mitigation, and Response.* Boca Raton, FL: CRC Press.

Edwards, J. (2009). Sinners in the Hands of an Angry God. In G. Perkins, & B. Perkins (Eds.), *The American Tradition in Literature* (12th ed., Vol. I, pp. 262-273). New York: McGraw-Hill.

Ehrenfeld, R. (2003). *Funding Evil: How Terrorism is Financed -- and How to Stop it.* Chicago: Bonus Books.

Ellis, J. W. (2007). *Police Analysis and Planning for Homicide Bombings: Prevention, Defense, and Response.* Springfield, IL: Charles C. Thomas Publisher, Ltd.

Ellis, R. E. (2011). *China-Latin America Military Engagement: Good Will, Good Business, and Strategic Position.* Carlisle, PA: Strategic Studies Institute.

Emerson, S. (2002). *American Jihad: The Terrorists Living Amongst Us.* New York: The Free Press.

Eshel, D. (2007, December). Defeating IEDs. *The Journal of Electronic Defense,* pp. 38-42.

Fandy, M. (2007). Enriched Islam: The Muslim Crisis of Education. *Survival,* 77-98.

Fay, J. J. (2011). *Contemporary security management* (Third ed.). Burlington, MA: Buttersworth-Heinemann.

Felbab-Brown, V. (2009). *The Violent Drug Market in Mexico and Lessons from Colombia.* Washington: Brookings Institute.

Ferguson, C. D., & Potter, W. C. (2004). *Improvised Nuclear Devices and Nuclear Terrorism.* Stockholm: The Weapons of Mass Destruction Commission.

Fishel, J. T., & Manwaring, M. G. (2006). *Uncomfortable Wars Revisited.* Norman, OK: University of Oklahoma Press.

Flanigan, S. T., & Abdel-Samad, M. (2009). Hezbollah's Social Jihad: Nonprofits as Resistance Organizations. *Middle East Policy, XVI*(2), 122-137.

Fowler, M. C. (2005). *Amateur Soldiers, Global Wars: Insurgency and Modern Conflict.* Westport, CT: Praeger Security International.

Fowler, W. (2005). *The Special Forces Guide to Escape and Evasion.* New York: Thomas Dunne Books.

Frey, B. S. (2007). *Why Kill Politicians? A Rational Choice Analysis of Political Assassinations.* Basel: Center for Research in Economics, Management and the Arts.

Gabriel, M. A. (2006). *Journey into the Mind of an Islamic Terrorist.* Lake Mary, Florida: Front Line.

Gander, T. (1990). *Guerrilla Warfare Weapons: The Modern Underground Fighter's Armoury.* New York: Sterling Publishing Co., Inc.

Garner, R. J. (1990). *Ethical Guidelines for Military Covert Operations.* Carlisle Barracks, Pennsylvania: U.S. Army War College.

Gerges, F. (2006). *Journey of the Jihadist: Inside Muslim Militancy.* Orlando: Harcourt.

Glasstone, S., & Dolan, P. J. (1977). *The Effects of Nuclear Weapons* (Third Edition ed.). Washington: United States Department of Defense; United States Department of Energy.

Glazebrook, J., & Nicholson, N. (2003). *Executive Protection Specialist Handbook* (Second Edition ed.). Shawnee Mission, Kansas: Varro Press.

Godlewski, R. (2008). Cultivating Creativity within Intelligence Analysis. *American Intelligence Journal, 25*(2), 85-87.

Godlewski, R. (2009). Human Intelligence: Perceiving an Enemy's Thoughts. *American Intelligence Journal, 27*(1), 29-37.

Godlewski, R. (2011). Financial Counterintelligence: Fractioning the Lifeblood of Asymmetrical Warfare. *American Intelligence Journal, 29*(2), 24-33.

Godlewski, R. (2011). Latte Intelligence: The Divorce of Shock Creativity and Special Information Operations. *American Intelligence Journal, 29*(1), 70-79.

Godlewski, R. (2012). *Mini-Manual of the Independent Counterterrorist* (Second ed.). Charleston, SC: CreateSpace Independent Publishing Platform.

Godlewski, R. (2012). *Skills of the Assassin: Understanding the Tactics of the Professional Killer.* Charleston: CreateSpace Independent Publishing Platform.

Godson, R. (2008). *Dirty Tricks or Trump Cards: U.S. Cover Action & Counterintelligence.* New Brunsick (U.S.A.): Transaction Publishers.

Goodman, M. (2007). *Rome and Jerusalem: The Clash of Ancient Civilizations.* New York: Alfred A. Knopf.

Gourevitch, P. (1998). *We wish to inform you that tomorrow we will be killed with our families.* New York: Picador.

Gray, C. S. (2006). *Another Bloody Century: Future Warfare.* London: Phoenix.

Grayson, G. W. (2010). *La Familia Drug Cartel: Implications for U.S.-Mexican Security.* Carlisle, PA: Strategic Studies Institute.

Griffin, J. (2010, November 19). *Foxs News* . Retrieved November 19, 2010, from http://www.foxnews.com/us/2010/11/19/ame ricas-third-war-mapping-mexican-drug-cartels/?test=latestnews

Gross, M. L. (2010). *Moral Dilemmas of Modern War: Torture, Assassination, and Blackmail in an Age of Asymmetric Conflict.* New York: Cambridge University Press.

Grossman, D. (2009). *On Killing: The Psychological Cost of Learning to Kill in War and Society* (Revised ed.). New York: Back Bay Books.

Grossman, D. A. (1993). Defeating the Enemy's Will: The Psychological Foundations of Maneuver Warfare. In J. e. Richard D. Hooker, *Maneuver Warfare: An Anthology*. Novato, CA: Presidio Press.

Guevara, C. (1961). *Guerrilla Warfare*. New York: Monthly Review Press.

Gurr, T. R. (1998). Terrorism in democracies: Its social and political bases. In W. Reich, *Origins of Terrorism: Psychologies, Ideologies, Theologies, States of Mind* (pp. 86-102). Washington: Woodrow Wilson Center Press.

Hamilton, S. (2009, November). Cyber Threats: We don't know what we don't know. *Armed Forces Journal*, pp. 33-34, 41.

Harclerode, P. (2000). *Secret Soldiers: Special Forces in the War Against Terrorism*. London: Cassell & Company.

Hayes, S. K. (1981). *The Ninja and their secret fighting art*. Rutland, VT: Charles E. Tuttle Company.

Headquarters, Department of the Army. (2002). *FM 3-06 Combined Arms Operations in Urban Terrain*. Washington: Department of the Army.

Heiden, K. (1944). *Der Fuehrer: Hitler's rise to power*. Boston: Houghton Mifflin Company.

Herzog, C. (1982). *The Arab-Israeli Wars: War and Peace in the Middle East from the War of Independence through Lebanon*. New York: Vintage.

Hoffman, B. (2006). A Nasty Business. In R. D. Howard, & R. L. Sawyer, *Terrorism and Counterterrorism: Understanding the New Security Environment: Readings and Interpretations* (pp. 402-407). Dubuque, Iowa: McGraw-Hill.

Hoffman, F. G. (2007, April). Mind Maneuvers: The Psychological Element of Counterinsurgency Warfare can be the Most Persuasive. *Armed Forces Journal*, pp. 28-32.

Holder, P. T., & Hawley, D. L. (1998). *The Executive Protection Professional's Manual*. Boston: Butterworth-Heinemann.

Howard, R. D. (2007). *Intelligence in Denied Areas: New Concepts for a Changing Security Environment*. Hurlbert Field: Joint Special Operations University.

Hristov, J. (2010). Self-Defense Forces, Warlords, or Criminal Gangs? Towards a New Conceptualization of Paramilitarism in Colombia. *Labour, Capital & Society, 43*(2), 14-56.

Hughes, D. (1996). When terrorists go nuclear. *Popular Mechanics*, pp. 56-59.

Hunter, T. B. (2009). *Targeted Killing: Self-Defense, Preemption, and the War on Terrorism*. Lexington, KY: BookSurge.

Hurth, J. D. (2012). *Combat Tracking Guide*. Mechanicsburg, PA: Stackpole Books.

Ibrahim, R. (2009). *War and Peace -- and Deceit -- in Islam*. Pajamas Media.

Jabber, P. (1986). Egypt's Crisis, America's Dilemma. *Foreign Affairs*, 960-980.

Jaber, H. (1997). *Hezbollah: Born with a Vengeance.* New York: Columbia University Press.

Joes, A. J. (2007). *Urban Guerrilla Warfare.* Lexington: University Press of Kentucky.

Jones, A. (2004). Parainstitutional Violence in Latin America. *Latin American Politics and Society, 46*(4), 127-148.

Jones, A., Kovacich, G. l., & Luzwick, P. G. (2002). *Global Information Warfare: How Businesses, Governments, and Others Achieve Objectives and Attain Competitive Advantages.* New York: Auerbach.

Jones, I. (2010). *The Human Factor: Inside the CIA's Dysfunctional Intelligence Culture.* New York: Encounter Books.

Kahaner, L. (2007). *AK-47: The weapon that changed the face of war.* Hoboken: John Wiley & Sons, Inc.

Kan, P. R. (2008). *Drug Intoxicated Irregular Fighters: Complications, Dangers, and Responses.* Carlisle, PA: Strategic Studies Institute.

Kan, P. R. (2011). *Mexico's "Narco-Refugees": The Looming Challenge for U.S. National Security.* Carlisle, PA: Strategic Studies Institute.

Kay, C. (2001). Reflections on Rual Violence in Latin America. *Third World Quarterly, 22*(5), 741-775.

Kellner, T., & Pipitone, F. (2010). Inside Mexico's Drug War. *World Policy Journal*, 29-37.

Kenney, M. (2007). *From Pablo to Osama: Trafficking and Terrorist Networks, Government Bureaucracies, and Competitive Adaptation.* University Park, PA: The Pennsylvania State University Press.

Kenney, M. (2007). The Architecture of Drug Trafficking: Network Forms of Organisation in the Colombian Cocaine Trade. *Global Crime,* 8(3), 233-259.

Kennison, P., & Loumansky, A. (2007). Shoot to kill -- understanding police use of force in combatting suicide terrorism. *Crime, Law, and Social Change, 47*(3), 151-168.

Khosrokhavar, F. (2005). *Suicide Bombers: Allah's New Martyrs.* London: Pluto Press.

Kiernan, K. L. (2009). Counterintelligence and Law Enforcement. In J. E. Sims, & B. Gerber, *Vaults, Mirrors, & Masks: Rediscovering U.S. Counterintelligence* (pp. 149-171). Washington: Georgetown University Press.

Klein, A. J. (2007). *Striking Back: The 1972 Munich Olympics Massacre and Israel's Deadly Response.* New York: Random House.

Kouzminov, A. (2005). *Biological Espionage: Special Operations of the Soviet and Russian Foreign Intelligence Services in the West.* London: Greenhill Books.

Kovats-Bernat, J. C. (2006). Factional Terror, Paramilitarism and Civil War in Haiti: The View from Port-au-Prince, 1994-2004. *Anthropologia, 48,* 117-139.

Krepinevich, A. F. (2010). *7 Deadly Scenarios: A Military Futurist Explores War in the Twenty-First Century.* New York: Bantam Books.

Kushner, H., & Davis, B. (2004). *Holy War on the Home Front: The Secret Islamic Terror Network in the United States.* New York: Sentinel.

Lambakis, S. J. (2004). Reconsidering Asymmetric Warfare. *Joint Force Quarterly,* 102-108.

Lance, P. (2003). *1000 years for revenge: International terrorism and the FBI -- the untold story.* New York: Regan Books.

Lawrence, E. (2005). *Tactical Pistol Shooting.* Iola, WI: Gun Digest Books.

Lawrence, T. (1935). *Seven Pillars of Wisdom.* New York: Doubleday, Doran & Company, Inc.

Lee, G. D. (2004). *Global Drug Enforcement: Practical Investigative Techniques.* Boca Raton, FL: CRC Press.

Leebaert, D. (2006). *To Dare and to Conquer: Special Operations and the Destiny of Nations from Achilles to Al Qaeda.* New York: Back Bay Books.

Mabon, S. (2012). The Battle for Bahrain: Iranian-Saudi Rivalry. *Middle East Policy, 19*(2), 84-97. Retrieved October 11, 2012

Mack, J. (1996). *Running a Ring of Spies: Spycraft and Black Operations in the Real World of Espionage.* Boulder: Paladin Press.

Magee, A. C. (2009, Winter). Counterintelligence in Irregular Warfare: A Void in the Full-Spectrum Joint Force Capability. *American Intelligence Journal*, pp. 54-60.

Manwaring, M. G. (2009). *A "New" Dynamic in the Western Hemisphere Security Environment: The Mexican Zetas and Other Private Armies.* Carlisle: Strategic Studies Institute.

Marcella, G. (2008). *War without Borders: The Colombia-Ecuador Crisis of 2008.* Carlisle, PA: Strategic Studies Institute.

Marighella, C. (n.d.). *Mini-Manual of the Urban Guerrilla.*

Marks, T. A. (2007, March-April). A Model Counterinsurgency: Uribe's Colombia (2002-2006) vs FARC. *Military Review*, pp. 41-56.

Martines, L. (2012). Mexican Crime Cartels. *Journal of Counterterrorism & Homeland Security International, 18*(1), 36-40.

May, T. (2007). *THE MONGOL ART OF WAR: Chinggis Khan and the Mongol Military System* (Book Club ed.). Yardley, PA: Westholme Publishing.

McMains, M. J., & Mullins, W. C. (2010). *Crisis Negotiations: Managing Critical Incidents and Hostage Situations in Law Enforcement and Corrections* (4th ed.). New Providence, NJ: Matthew Bender & Company.

McNeill, W. H. (1993). Patterns of Disease Emergence in History. In S. S. Morse (Ed.), *Emerging Viruses* (pp. 29-36). New York: Oxford University Press.

McRaven, W. H. (1996). *SPEC OPS: Case Studies in Special Operations Warfare: Theory and Practice.* New York: Ballantine Books.

Melton, H. K., & Wallace, R. (2009). *The Official C.I.A. Manual of Trickery and Deception.* New York: William Morrow.

Mendell, R. L. (2011). *The Quiet Threat: Fighting Industrial Espionage in America* (Second ed.). Springfield, IL: Charles C. Thomas Publisher.

Merari, A. (1998). The readiness to kill and die: Suicidal terrorism in the Middle East. In W. Reich, *Origins of Terrorism: Psychologies, Ideologies, Theologies, States of Mind* (pp. 192-207). Washington: Woodrow Wilson Center Press.

Miller, C. R. (2005). *Electromagnetic Pulse Threats in 2010.* Maxwell AFB: Center for Strategy and Technology, Air War College/Air University.

Miller, R., & Kane, L. A. (2012). *Scaling Force: Dynamic Decision-making under Threat of Violence.* Wolfeboro, NH: YMAA Publication Center, Inc.

Minieri, M. W. (2004). *Protecting Corporate Secrets: A Brief Primer on Contemporary Practices in Information Security.* Reston: Kroll Schiff & Associates. Retrieved from http://www.krollworldwide.com

Morgan, F. E. (1992). *Living the Martial Way: A Manual for the Way a Modern Warrior Should Think.* Fort Lee, NJ: Barricade Books.

Morris, B. (1997). *Israel's Border Wars 1949-1956.* New York: Oxford University Press, Inc.

Murphy, M. N. (2010). *Small Boats, Weak States, Dirty Money: Piracy and Maritime Terrorism in the Modern World.* New York: Columbia University Press.

Musashi, M. (1645). The Book of Five Rings.

Nance, M. W. (2014). *Terrorist Recognition Handbook: A Practitioner's Manual for Predicting and Indentifying Terrorist Activities* (Third ed.). Boca Raton, FL: CRC Press.

Norell, J. O. (September). Are you an American or Are you a Terrorist? *America's 1st Freedom*, pp. 30-33, 56-57.

Nutt, S., & Lyons, J. (2008). *Virtual Worlds and Terrorist Attack Planning.* Shawnee, OK: Urban Warfare Analysis Center.

Oatman, R. L. (2006). *Executive Protection: New Solutions for a New Era.* Arnold, Maryland: Noble House.

O'Neill, B. E. (1978). *Armed Struggle in Palestine: A Political-Military Analysis.* Boulder: Westview Press.

Paladin Press. (1985). *Handbook for Volunteers of the Irish Republican Army.* Boulder, CO: Paladin Press.

Paladin Press. (1991). *Federal Bomb Intelligence: U.S. Government Guide to Terrorist Explosives.* Boulder: Paladin Press.

Paladin Press. (1993). *KGB Alpha Team Training Manual: How the Soviets Trained for Personal Combat, Assassination, and Subversion.* Boulder: Paladin Press.

Pelton, R. Y. (2007). *Licensed to Kill: Hired Guns in the War on Terror.* New York: Three Rivers Press.

Peters, R. (2006, December). Killing with Kindness: Political correctness infiltrates the Army. *Armed Forces Journal,* pp. 28-32.

Peters, R. (2007, January). Rebels and Religion: How fighters become fanatics. *Armed Forces Journal,* pp. 28-31.

Peters, R. (2007, September). When Muslim armies won: Lessons from yesteryears's jihadi victories. *Armed Forces Journal,* pp. 38-41,47.

Phalen, D. (2011). Protecting Those Who Save Lives. *The Journal of Counterterrorism & Homeland Security International, 17*(2), 24-26.

Piggott, L. (2005, Autumn). Tribalism in the Arab MENA Region. *Policy,* pp. 15-20.

Poole, H. J. (2003). *The Tiger's Way: A U.S. Private's Best Chance for Survival.* Emerald Isle, NC: Posterity Press.

Poole, H. J. (2004). *Tactics of the Crescent Moon: Militant Muslim Combat Methods.* Emerald Isle, North Carolina: Posterity Press.

Poole, H. J. (2005). *Militant Tricks: Battlefield Ruses of the Islamic Insurgent.* Emerald Isle, North Carolina: Posterity Press.

Poole, H. J. (2007). *Dragon Days: Time for "Unconventional" Tactics.* Emerald Isle, NC: Posterity Press.

Poole, H. J. (2008). *Tequila Junction: 4th-Generation Counterinsurgency.* Emerald Isle, NC: Posterity Press.

Poole, H. J. (2011). *Global Warrior: Averting WWIII.* Emerald Isle, NC: Posterity Press.

Porter, L. E. (2005). Policing the Police: Theoretical and Practical Contributions of Psychologists to Understanding and Preventing Corruption. In L. Alison (Ed.), *The Forensic Psychologist's Casebook: Psychological Profiling and Criminal Investigation* (pp. 143-169). New York: Routledge.

Powers Jr., J. F. (2006). *Filling Special Operations Gaps with Civilian Expertise.* Hurlburt Field: Joint Special Operations University.

Purpura, P. P. (2008). *Security and loss prevention: An introduction* (5th ed.). Burlington, MA: Elsevier Butterworth-Heinemann.

Rabinovich, A. (2004). *The Yom Kippur War: The Epic Encounter that Transformed the Middle East.* New York: Schocken.

Randal, J. (2004). *Osama: The Making of a Terrorist.* New York: Vintage Books.

Rashid, A. (2010). *Taliban: Militant Islam, Oil and Fundamentalism in Central Asia* (Second ed.). New Haven, CT: Yale University Press.

Rassler, D., & Brown, V. (2011). *The Haqqani Nexis and the Evolution of al-Qa'ida.* United States Military Academy. West Point: The Combating Terrorism Center at West Point.

Ratner, S. R. (2007). Predator and Prey: Seizing and Killing Suspected Terrorists Abroad. *The Journal of Political Philosophy, 15*(3), 251-275.

Rehov, P. (Producer), & Rehov, P. (Director). (2006). [Motion Picture].

Reisman, W. M., & Antoniou, C. T. (1994). *The Laws of War: A comprehensive collection of primary documents on international laws governing armed conflict.* New York: Random House.

Rooney, D. (2004). *Guerrilla: Insurgents, patriots, and terrorists from Sun Tzu to Bin Laden.* London: Brassey's.

Ross, J. F. (2009). *War on the Run: The Epic Story of Robert Rogers and the Conquest of America's First Frontier.* New York: Bantam Books.

Sabet, K., & Rios, V. (2009). *Why violence has increased in Mexico and what we can do about it.* Independent Report, Washington.

Schechter, E. (2008, November/December). Stopping IEDs: Gaming, training communities set up. *C4ISR Journal*, p. 18.

Schroen, G. C. (2007). *First In: An Isider's Account of How the CIA Spearheaded the War on Terror in Afghanistan.* New York: Ballantine Books.

Schweitzer, D. (2002). *Securing the Network from Malicious Code: A Complete Guide to Defending Against Viruses, Worms, and Trojans.* Indianapolis: Wiley Publishing, Inc.

Shulsky, A. N., & Schmitt, G. J. (2002). *Silent Warfare: Understanding the World of Intelligence* (Third Edition ed.). Washington: Potomac Books.

Shultz Jr., R. H. (2006). Showstoppers: Nine Reasons Why We Never Sent Our Special Operations Forces after al Qaeda before 9/11. In R. D. Howard, *Terrorism and Counterterrorism: Understanding the New Security Environment: Readings and Interpretations* (Second Edition ed., pp. 518-530). Dubuque, IA: McGraw-Hill.

Sikand, Y. (2007). Stoking the Flames: Intra-Muslim Rivalries in India and the Saudi Connection. *Comparative Studies of South Asia, Africa, and the Middle East, 27*(1), 95-108.

Sinno, A. H. (2008). *Organizations at War in Afghanistan and Beyond.* Ithaca, NY: Cornell University Press.

Sloan, S., & Bunker, R. J. (2011). *Red Teams and Counterterrorism Training.* Norman, OK: University of Oklahoma Press.

Smidt, C. E. (2005, Autumn). Religion and American Attitudes toward Islam and an Invasion of Iraq. *Sociology of Religion, 66*(3), pp. 243-261.

Smith, D. D. (2002). *Deterring America.* New York: Cambridge University Press.

Sockut, E. (1995). *Secrets of Street Survival -- Israeli Style: Staying alive in a Civilian War Zone.* Boulder: Paladin Press.

Spalding, R. (2010). *Drug Subs: The Worldwide Invasion by the Narco-Submarine Fleet.* Signal Mountain, TN: Spalding Publishing.

Spencer, R. (2006). *The Truth about Muhammad: Founder of the World's Most Intolerant Religion.* Washington: Regnery Publishing.

Sperry, P. (2005). *Infiltration: How Muslim Spies and Subversives have Penetrated Washington.* Nashville: Nelson Current.

Spicer, M. (2011). Mexican Drug Cartels: The Growing Threat of the Sniper Attack. *Journal of Counterterrorism & Homeland Security International, 16*(4), 48-50.

Sprinzak, E. (1998). The psychopolitical formation of extreme left terrorism in a democracy: The case of the Weathermen. In W. Reich, *Origins of Terrorism: Psychologies, Ideologies, Theologies, States of Mind* (pp. 65-85). Washington: Woodrow Wilson Center Press.

Spulak Jr., R. G. (2007). *A Theory of Special Operations: The Origin, Qualities, and Use of SOF.* Hurlburt Field: Joint Special Operations University.

Steele, R. D. (2010). *Human Intelligence: All Humans, All Minds, All the Time.* Carlisle, PA: Strategic Studies Institute.

Stojkovic, S., Kalinich, D., & Klofas, J. (2012). *Criminal Justice Organizations: Administration and Management* (Fifth Edition ed.). Belmont, CA: Wadsworth.

Sullivan, J. P., & Elkus, A. (2011, July 14). Narco-Armor in Mexico. *Small Wars Journal.*

Summers Jr, H. G. (1982). *On Strategy: A Critical Analysis of the Vietnam War.* New York: Presidio Press.

Swanson, S. (2007, January-February). Know Your Enemy: Human Intelligence Key to SOF Missions. *Special Warfare*, pp. 16-24.

Swanson, S. (2007, May). Viral Targeting of the IED Social Network System. *Small Wars Journal*, pp. 2-16.

Taber, R. (2002). *War of the Flea: The Classic Study of Guerrilla Warfare.* Washington: Potomac Books.

Tatar, B. (2005). Emergence of Nationalist Identity in Armed Insurrections: A Comparison of Iraq and Nicaragua. *Anthropological Quarterly*, 179-195.

The Seven Military Classics of Ancient China. (1993). (R. D. Sawyer, Trans.) Boulder: Westview Press.

Thomas, T. L. (2005). Russian Tactical Lessons Learned Fighting Chechen Separatists. *Journal of Slavic Military Studies, 18*, pp. 731-766.

Thurman, J. T. (2006). *Practical Bomb Scene Investigation.* Boca Raton, FL: CRC Press.

Tierney, J. (2012, March). Know Thy Enemy's Weapons: The Army Needs to Step Up Training on Foreign Arms. *Armed Forces Journal*, 8-10,30.

Timmerman, K. R. (2006). *Countdown to Crisis: The Coming Nuclear Showdown with Iran.* New York: Three Rivers Press.

Tomajczyk, S. F. (1999). *Bomb Squads.* Osceola, WI: MBI Publishing.

Toolis, K. (1995). *Rebel Hearts: Journeys Within the IRA's Soul.* New York: St. Martin's Griffin.

Tse-tung, M. (2009). *On Guerrilla Warfare.* New York: Classic House Books.

Tucker, D. (1998, Summer). Fighting Barbarians. *Parameters*, pp. 69-79.

Tucker, J. B. (2006). *War of Nerves: Chemical Warfare from World War I to Al-Qaeda.* New York: Pantheon.

Turbiville Jr., G. H. (2007). *Hunting Leadership Targets in Counterinsurgency and Counterterrorist Operations: Selected Perspectives and Experiences*. Hurlbert Field: Joint Special Operations University.

Turbiville Jr., G. H. (2009). *Guerrilla Counterintelligence: Insurgent Approaches to Neutralizing Adversary Intelligence Operations*. Hurlburt Field: Joint Special Operations University.

U.S. Army Training and Doctrine Command. (2003). *A Military Guide to Terrorism in the Twenty-First Century*. Fort Leavenworth: Deputy Chief of Staff for Intelligence.

U.S. Department of Defense. (2001, April 12). Dictionary of Military and Associated Terms. *Joint Publication 1-02*. Washington: Department of Defense.

Ulrichsen, K. C. (2009, Summer). Internal and External Security in the Arab Gulf States. *Middle East Policy, XVI*(2), 39-58.

United States Army. (2005). *FMI 3-34.119 Improvised Explosive Device Defeat*. Fort Leonard Wood: Department of the Army.

United States Catholic Conference, Inc. (1994). *Catechism of the Catholic Church*. New York: Doubleday.

United States Department of Homeland Security. (2008). *Terrorist Weaponization of Fire: Improvised Incendiary Devices (IID) and Arson*. Transportation Security Administration, Office of Intelligence. Washington: U.S. Government.

United States Department of the Army. (1961). *FM 31-21 Guerrilla Warfare and Special Forces Operations*. Washington: U.S. War Office.

United States Marine Corps. (1988). *FRONT-LINE INTELLIGENCE*. Washington: Department of the Navy.

Vacca, J. R. (2002). *Computer Forensics: Computer Crime Scene Investigation*. Hingham, MA: Charles River Media, Inc.

Velocity, M. (2012). *Rapid Fire! Tactics for High Threat, Protection and Combat Operations*. Lexington, KY: Max Velocity.

Venter, A. J. (2007). *Allah's Bomb: The Islamic Quest for Nuclear Weapons*. Guilford, CT: The Lyons Press.

Venter, A. J. (2008). *War Dog: Fighting Other People's Wars: The Modern Mercenary in Combat*. Drexel Hill, PA: Casemate Publishing.

Waisberg, T. (2009). The Colombia-Ecuador Armed Crisis of March 2008: The Practice of Targeted Killing and Incursions against Non-State Actors Harbored at Terrorist Safe Havens in a Third Party State. *Studies in Conflict & Terrorism, 32*, 476-488.

Watkins, L. J. (2011). *Self-propelled Semi-submersibles: The Next Great Threat to Regional Security and Stability*. Monterey: Naval Post-Graduate School. Retrieved October 12, 2012, from http://calhoun.nps.edu/public/bitstream/handle/10945/5629/11Jun_Watkins.pdf?sequence=1

Waugh, B., & Keown, T. (2004). *Hunting the Jackal.* New York: Avon Books.

West, J. (2008). *Fry the Brain: The Art of Urban Sniping and its Role in Modern Guerrilla Warfare.* Countryside, VA: SSI.

Wilkinson, P. (1986). *Terrorism & the Liberal State* (Second Edition ed.). New York: New York University Press.

Williams, P. (2009). *Criminals, Militias, and Insurgents: Organized Crime in Iraq.* Carlisle, PA: Strategic Studies Institute.

Williams, P., & Felbab-Brown, V. (2012). *Drug Trafficking, Violence, and Instability.* Carlisle, PA: Strategic Studies Institute.

Wilson, B. (2011). Submersibles and Transnational Criminal Organizations. *Ocean and Coastal Law Journal,* 35-63.

Wimberley, S. (1997). *Special Forces Guerrilla Warfare Manual.* Boulder: Paladin Press.

Zuhur, S. (2008). *HAMAS and ISRAEL: Conflicting Strategies of Group-Based Politics.* Carlisle, PA: Strategic Studies Institute.

ABOUT THE AUTHOR

R.J. Godlewski (Pronounced *GOD LESS KEY*) is the chief executive manager for a threat resolution services company and serves as president of an international security corporation practicing Fourth-Generation Corporate Security (4GCS) doctrine. He holds an M.A. in Military Studies, Asymmetrical Warfare and a B.A. in Intelligence Studies, Terrorism Studies, both of which earned with honors from American Military University. Mr. Godlewski also holds formal academic training in explosive ordnance disposal and security management and is an honorably discharged veteran of the U.S. Navy and U.S. Navy Reserve.

His previous books include:

Fourth-Generation Corporate Security: Asymmetrical Warfare for Protective Services Professionals

Mini-Manual of the Independent Counterterrorist, Third Edition

Skills of the Assassin: Understanding the Tactics of the Professional Killer

Targeting Narco-Submarine Networks through Deep Penetration, Autonomous Maritime Irregular Warfare Units Operating within a Hunter-Killer Role

www.ingramcontent.com/pod-product-compliance
Lightning Source LLC
Chambersburg PA
CBHW020314290526
45785CB00007B/2793